Faith Styles

Other books by John R. Mabry

The Way of Thomas:
Nine Insights for Enlightened Living from the Secret Sayings of Jesus

Noticing the Divine:
An Introduction to Interfaith Spiritual Guidance

God Has One Eye:
The Mystics of the World's Religions

God is a Great Underground River:
Articles, Essays, and Homilies
on Interfaith Spirituality

I believe in a God Who is Growing:
Process Perspectives on the Creed,
the Sacraments, and the Christian Life

Who Are the Independent Catholics?
An Introduction to the Independent
and Old Catholic Churches
(With John P. Plummer)

Crisis and Communion:
The Re-Mythologization of the Eucharist

Heretics, Mystics, & Misfits

God As Nature Sees God:
A Christian Reading of the Tao Te Ching

The Tao Te Ching: A New Translation

The Little Book of the Tao Te Ching

Faith Styles

Ways People Believe

JOHN R. MABRY

MOREHOUSE PUBLISHING
HARRISBURG–NEW YORK

Morehouse Publishing, P.O. Box 1321, Harrisburg, PA 17105

Morehouse Publishing, 445 Fifth Avenue, New York, NY 10016

Morehouse Publishing is an imprint of Church Publishing Incorporated.

Cover design by Lee Singer

Library of Congress Cataloging-in-Publication Data

Mabry, John R.
Faith styles : ways people believe / by John R. Mabry.
p. cm.
ISBN-13: 978-0-8192-2222-0 (pbk.)
1. Spirituality. 2. Spiritual life. 3. Faith. 4. Religions. I. Title.
BL624.M27 2006
204'.2--dc22

2006023501

Printed in the United States of America

06 07 08 09 10 9 8 7 6 5 4 3 2 1

This book is dedicated to my father,

RUSSEL B. MABRY,

who first taught me to
think critically about religion

Contents

Introduction

"How arrogant!" a woman in my class exclaimed. I was taken aback, and for a couple of seconds that seemed like hours, I came up speechless. I had been teaching a class on faith development theory and was quickly rushing through Fowler's six stages. But because in my experience students find Fowler baroque and difficult to grasp, I had quickly turned my attention to Scott Peck's simplified model (explicated below). Once they had grasped the basics, my students (as they are wont to do) rebelled, leading to the show-stopping exclamation. "That's hierarchical!" she continued. "It assumes that stage three is superior to stage two, and stage four is better than all of them!" I had no rebuttal to offer, because I agreed with her.

"This system is not perfect," I admitted, "but I will ask you to bear with me, because it is simply the best tool we have for the job right now." Grumbling a little, they settled in to discussing the usefulness of Peck's model in assessing clients and informing the spiritual guidance process. Their reaction stuck with me, though, and for years I have been thinking, "There must be better model."

Coming up empty-handed, I asked a colleague, Jürgen Schwing, to teach the next class on this subject. Dispensing with Fowler and Peck, he presented a model of his own, designed to eschew the hierarchical nature of the previous models. But again, the students felt the model unfair to more traditional believers. I watched Jürgen shift uncomfortably during the dissent, much as

I had done myself. But I was inspired by his system, and building upon it, the Faith Styles model emerged.

This book is an attempt to describe a model of spiritual assessment that is both non-developmental and non-hierarchical in nature. In developing it I am indebted to Fowler, Peck, my friend Jürgen Schwing, my clients, and most especially my students, without whom there would have been no necessity mothering this invention.

Previous Models

To fully understand the foundations of the Faith Styles system, a brief overview of antecendent models is in order. Each of them has contributed significantly to my understanding of religious typology, and has important similarities to the styles reflected in the Faith Styles model.

James Fowler's Stages of Faith. James Fowler, PhD, is a developmental psychologist, a United Methodist layperson, and director of the Center for Faith Development at Emory University. He is a pioneer of faith development theory, and his book *Stages of Faith* (San Francisco: HarperSanFrancisco, 1995) is a classic. Fowler identifies six faith stages through which most people travel.

The first stage Fowler calls "Intuitive-Projective" faith. It usually occurs between the ages of three and seven and is characterized by the psyche's unprotected exposure to the unconscious. Imagination runs wild in this stage, uninhibited by logic. It is the first step in self-awareness, and the time when one absorbs one's culture's strong taboos. The advantages of this stage are the birth of imagination and the growing ability to grasp and unify one's perception of reality. Stage one is also dangerous, though, in that the child's imagination can be "possessed" by unrestrained images of terror and destruction from the unconscious. There is also the danger of exploitation of the fertile imagination by enforced taboos and indoctrination.

The second stage is called "Mythic-Literal" faith, in which symbol and ritual begin to be integrated by the child. These symbols, however, are one-dimensional, and only literal interpretations of myth and symbol are possible. The runaway imagination of stage one is here harnessed, and linear thinking becomes normative. Found mostly in school children (although one can maintain this state for life), stage two persons have a strong belief in the justice and reciprocity of the universe, and the Divine is almost always anthropomorphic. Objective distance and critical evaluation of myth or symbology is impossible.

The third stage is labeled "Synthetic-Conventional" faith. The majority of the population finds its permanent home in this stage. Usually arising in adolescence, this stage demands a complex pattern of socialization and integration, and faith is an inseparable factor in the ordering of one's world. It is a stage characterized by conformity, where one finds one's identity by aligning oneself with a certain perspective, and one lives directly through this perception with little opportunity to reflect on it critically. One has an ideology at this point, but may not be aware that one has it. Those who differ in opinion are seen as "the Other." Authority derives from the top down and is invested with power by majority opinion.

The fourth stage is known as "Individuative-Reflective." This is primarily a stage of angst and struggle, in which one must face difficult questions regarding identity and belief. Those who pass into stage four usually do so in their mid-thirties to early forties. At this time, the personality gradually detaches from the defining group from which it formerly drew its identity. The person is aware of him or herself as an individual and must—perhaps for the first time—take personal responsibility for his/her beliefs and feelings. This is a stage of demythologizing, where what was once unquestioned is now subjected to critical scrutiny. Stage four is heavily existential, where nothing is certain but one's own existence, and disillusionment reigns.

Stage five, "Conjunctive" faith, moves one from stage four's rationalism to the acknowledgment of paradox and transcendence. In this stage a person grasps the reality behind the symbols of his or her inherited systems, and is also drawn to and acknowledges the symbols of others' systems. This stage makes room for mystery and the unconscious and is fascinated by it while at the same time apprehensive of its power. It sees the power behind the metaphors while simultaneously acknowledging their relativity. In stage five, the world, demythologized in stage four, is resacralized, literally brimming with vision. It is also imbued with a new sense of justice that goes beyond justice as defined by one's own culture and people. Because one has begun to see "the bigger picture" the walls culture and tradition have built between ourselves and others begin to erode. It is not easy to live on the cusp of paradox, and due to its radical drive toward inclusivity, the mind struggles to assimilate and integrate faster than it can work through its cultural and psychological baggage. It is an overwhelming, ecstatic stage in which one is radically opened to possibility and wonder.

Stage six, the final stage, Fowler calls "Universalizing" faith. While in the previous stage, one glimpses a unitive view of reality, but feels torn between possibility and loyalty, and may even neglect to act on this new understanding out of a regard for self-preservation. In stage six, any such apprehensions dissolve, and one becomes an activist for the unitive vision. Stage six is the home of the true mystic, for whom all paths are valid paths, and the Divine is both imminent and transcendent.

M. Scott Peck's A Different Drum. Fowler's theory is complex, but Scott Peck has done an excellent job of simplifying it in his book *A Different Drum* (New York: Simon & Schuster, 1987). Very briefly, this model asserts that we begin life in a state of "chaos"—nobody but us exists, and we have no moral center. Most young children feel they are the center of the universe and are oblivious to the needs of others. Some people spend their lives in this first stage of development, although many who are stuck here into adulthood end up in prison. Peck calls stage one "Chaotic-Antisocial."

Most of us, however, at an appropriate age, move on to stage two, which Peck calls "Formal-Institutional" faith. This stage has very clear rules and regulations, a black and white system of morality, and a clearly defined system of orthodoxy to keep people on the straight and narrow. For people who have lived much of their lives in the chaos of stage one, stage two is a very real salvation—the structure of such a faith rescues them from their own headlong plunge toward self-destruction. Stage two faith is appropriate for older children and most adults. The great majority of religious people the world over live and die in stage two, and it serves them very well indeed.

For some, however, the rigidity and contradictions inherent in orthodoxy become too much to bear, and they begin to ask questions. What if the priests or the gurus or the imams are wrong? What if they are lying to us? What if they are simply ignorant and are stumbling around in the dark like the rest of us? The person who asks such questions has moved into stage three, "Skeptical-Individual" faith, the stage of questioning and doubt. This is a very valuable stage, where idols are smashed, worldviews discarded, and one's true seeking begins. Even though this is a very uncomfortable place to be, many people spend their lives here, and find meaning in their lives as activists, philosophers, or humanists. For them life is a question that has no answer, and yet the question itself contains sufficient substance to sustain them.

But beyond questioning lies another stage, where all the questions dissolve into silence. The fourth stage of faith is "Mystic-Communal"—where one has fallen in love with Mystery, that Mystery at the heart of all things. In this place one does not need questions, nor does one need answers. The religious traditions of the world are revealed to be arbitrary symbol sets, which are but fingers pointing at a reality that cannot be described, let alone comprehended, but can be experienced and participated in. In this stage, all divisions are illusory, and the distinctions between the universal and the particular disappear.

Jürgen Schwing's "Spiritual Care Assessment Model."[1] Schwing's model attempts to address the hierarchy implied in the previous two systems. He calls his categories "orientations" and defines them thusly:

> **The Humanist** regards the human spirit as the highest value. He or she doesn't see a need for a God or higher being. The humanist bases his or her knowledge on what can be perceived through ordinary human experience.
>
> **The Theist** believes in a personal God. He or she bases his values and decisions on faith in God who is revealed in a sacred scripture. The Christian looks to the Bible, the Jew to the Torah, the Muslim to the Qur'an for guidance. They all believe in a personal God who is the Supreme Being.
>
> **The Spiritual Person** (or **Spiritual Eclectic**) believes that there is a Higher Being, a divine reality, Spirit, Soul, or God. However, he or she doesn't derive knowledge primarily from revealed scriptures, but direct experience of the sacred. Other than the Humanist, the Spiritual Person allows for more than ordinary experience and acknowledges that transcendent experience of the sacred is possible and valid.
>
> **The Mystic** is someone who pursues higher states of consciousness or being that allow for a direct experience of the Divine or Ultimate

1. Unpublished handout—used by permission.

> Reality. For the mystic the Divine is a powerful presence that gives him or her deep knowledge and trust that all of life is sacred and every moment infused with Spirit.

While the insights of the developmental models by Fowler and Peck are valuable, they are of limited value in ministry because of the implied value that higher stages have over lower ones. The great advantage of Schwing's model is that it dispenses with the developmental underpinnings and regards categories of faith as being of equal value. The Faith Styles system is indebted to Schwing's approach, and is an expansion of it.

The Importance of a Model

When clients enter the room for spiritual guidance, they and their guides usually spend the first couple of sessions getting to know each other. During this time, the guide, while outwardly gathering information, is also inwardly making assessments that will determine to some degree how he or she will approach the guidance process. As we shall see, people have a variety of faith styles. Each of these styles differ from one another in key ways, and such differences, by necessity, will influence how the spiritual guide goes about his or her work, what recommendations are likely to be made, and even how the client's progress is to be assessed.

An assessment model will best serve spiritual guides if it does not assume the superiority of one style over another. Every person's relationship with Divinity is holy, regardless of how he or she views the Divine or his or her relationship with it. All people can experience growth and greater connection to the Divine and their communities, and it is not the job of spiritual guides to judge the propriety of one style over another. It is no doubt true that we will feel more comfortable with clients whose faith styles reflect our own, and in fact we may find that we are best at guiding people of some styles while we are utterly incapable of guiding people of other styles. This is simply a fact, and there is no shame in it. Rare indeed is the spiritual guide who can companion people of every faith style with equal efficacy. But this is another apology for such a model: without the ability to quickly assess a client's style of faith, it will take us longer to determine whether or not we will be a good fit. Being familiar with a model such as Faith Styles will help us to quickly and easily assess a client, usually within the first or second session, whereupon we may better be able to determine if the match is a good one, how to best proceed with the work, or whether to refer the client to someone with expertise in his or her faith style.

Each style carries with it certain assumptions about the Divine and the life of faith that will impact one's client. In our discussions of the various styles, we will focus on eight key questions: (1) How is the Divine imaged?(2) What is the nature of one's relationship with the Divine? (3) How does one construct meaning in the world? (4) What are the accepted sources of spiritual wisdom? (5) How is spiritual growth assessed? (6) What spiritual disciplines and practices are honored? (7) What are the advantages of the style? (8) What are the disadvantages?[2]

I have divided people into six broad styles, arranged in a wheel. I will discuss the six styles in two sections, first addressing what I call the primary triangle that represents the greatest diversity in the faith styles, and next the secondary triangle representing those styles that fall in between the points of the primary triangle. Following a description of each style, I will discuss how the eight defining questions are answered, drawing on the responses from a survey as my primary source.

Methodology and Language

These surveys were sent around the world, via e-mail to people of diverse faith traditions. Literally thousands of people saw my request, and about fifty completed the survey. Respondants were Buddhists, Catholics, Jews, mainline Christians, Evangelicals, Unitarian Universalists, and various brands of atheists, agnostics, and humanists. Although hundreds of Muslims, Hindus, Jains, and Sikhs were approached for this study, not a single one returned a completed survey form. I am sad not to have their experiences represented in this project. Except for people who wanted specific pseudonymns, I have changed all of the names to preserve the participants' anonymity.

The case studies presented in the first six chapters are composite characters derived from spiritual guidance clients I have had, parishioners I have counseled, and people I have known, while the examples in chapter eight are all illustrative fictions. In seminar demonstrations of this material, it has

2. Numbers 1, 3, and 4 are inspired by Schwing's "Spiritual Care Assessment Model."

been pointed out that the examples employ more of the directive method than the non-directive method currently in vogue in spiritual direction training programs. While I favor the non-directive method in my own practice, it is also true that the directive method is unduly maligned and often appropriate. It was appropriate in my examples because I have a very short space in which to illustrate my points, and cannot take thirty pages of dialog that the non-directive method by necessity entails without unnecessarily taxing the reader. Please keep in mind that what I am illustrating in these examples are styles of faith, not spiritual direction techniques.

Each example is presented as a random and arbitrary example and is not to be thought of as being in any way definitive. Instead, each example merely represents how one individual belonging to each of the six categories might sound, with full awareness that for every category there are millions of stories.

Each chapter closes with a handy "At-a-Glance" chart for quick reference.

Faith Styles is written primarily with spiritual directors in mind, but also with attention to other helping professions that might reasonably consider themselves to be offering spiritual guidance: pastors, rabbis, chaplains, and other clergy; psychotherapists, life coaches, social workers, and pastoral counselors, among others.

Because of this broad approach, and also because the majority of spiritual directors are unhappy with the misleading and often inaccurate moniker "spiritual *director*," I have referred to helping professionals in this book as "spiritual guides," and those they serve as "clients." Though I realize there are many in the spiritual direction community who object to the latter term because they fear it points to an unwelcome professionalization of the ministry, I have adopted it here for a couple of reasons. First and foremost, I hesitate to use the word "directee" because it is such a proprietary word, existing only within the literature of spiritual direction—plus, it is awkward and obfuscatory. On the other hand, "client" is far less clumsy and is easily understood by those of any helping profession. Fewer people, I predict, will be unhappy with the professional implications of "client" than will be uncomfortable with the weirdness of a term like "directee."

Please keep in mind that explications of each faith style are by necessity generalizations and will not perfectly describe everyone's faith style. It will, however, give us a general overview of how people inhabiting each style approach spirituality and how they might best be served by their spiritual guides.

The Primary Triangle

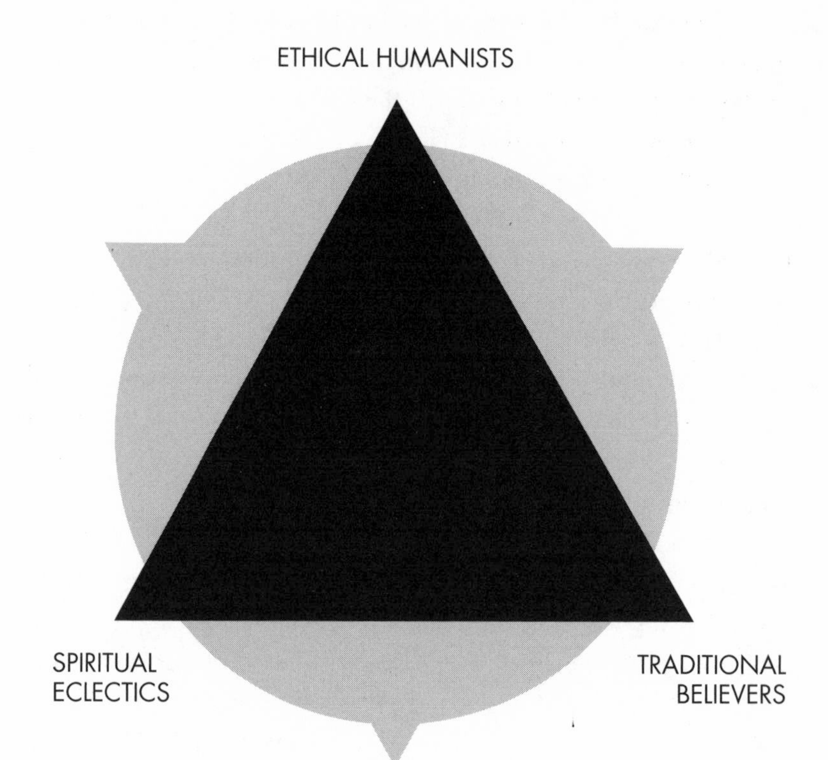

FIGURE 1: THE PRIMARY TRIANGLE

The primary triangle describes what we might consider the most obvious and mutually exclusive of the styles: Traditional Believers, Spiritual Eclectics, and Ethical Humanists.

1
Traditional Believers

When Becky showed up at her spiritual guidance session, she was positively shaking. She had missed her period and was certain that she was pregnant. She and her husband, Tom, were committed Roman Catholics and, as they believed they should, practiced the rhythm method of birth control. They had three children already and were struggling to make ends meet. The moment Becky was inside the meeting room, she broke down. Diane, her spiritual guide, worked hard to create safe space for her clients, and she sat quietly until Becky was calm enough to speak.

"Why would God do this to us?" she asked. "What does God want of us? What did we do to deserve this? How are we going to survive?" Diane maintained a compassionate presence and allowed Becky's questions to come out without attempting to answer them. After sitting together in silence for a while, Diane asked Becky, "Do you really think God is punishing you?"

"It feels like it. We *can't* have another child. It's not fair. We can barely pay our bills now, and we're so stretched to the limit sometimes Tom and I barely see each other before we collapse into bed at night."

"What does the Church say about children?"

"It says they are a blessing. And our children *have* been a blessing. But another one would. . . . I'm scared." In her head, Becky heard the scripture verse from Genesis, "Go forth and multiply," and suddenly saw hundreds of clones of her and Tom crowding her mind's eye. She shook her head to clear it of the image.

"Have you prayed about this? Have you told God how you feel?"

"No!" Becky said, with a tone that carried an unspoken, "Of course not!"

"Why not? Don't you think God cares how you feel?"

"I'm not sure . . . God's right, after all. And I'm . . . I'm not being very obedient." She started to cry again.

"How could you be disobedient? Have you done anything that the Church considers a sin?"

"Yes . . . no, I don't know. Isn't just being here and saying these things a rebellious spirit? I am not being an obedient daughter. I just want to be good, but it doesn't seem fair. Isn't God supposed to be fair?"

Diane let the question hang in the air and waited. "Who am I without God's love?" Becky continued, "How can I say 'no' to God? How could I live?"

Divine Image

Becky's crisis of faith reveals many fundamental elements of the Traditional Believer's faith style. Traditional Believers live in a universe that is highly structured. Divinity is all-powerful and in control of all things at all times. The Divine is usually imaged as male, often as a father figure, the head of a metaphorical family that extends to include each individual believer. In the above episode, Becky does not feel like an "obedient daughter" and probably understands that relationship literally.

Traditional images are often very human indeed, as those who responded to the survey make clear. Ruth, an Orthodox Jew from New Jersey, wrote of the Divine, "I suppose when I imagine him, he's the typical Judeo-Christian Rabbinic figure: long white beard, etc.—think Michelangelo's Moses." Ed, a Christian from Washington state, describes the Divine as "a male human figure (we were made in his image) that radiates light and warmth."

The Divine attribute stressed in the Traditional system is justice, and the deity holds a fine balance between judgment and mercy. For Traditional Believers this justice is maintained in that human beings have been given ample opportunity to avail themselves of grace and are usually fully aware of the consequences of rejecting the Divine plan for salvation. Thus, the Divine judges no one; people themselves choose salvation or damnation. As

Ed describes it, "Although [God] loves everyone more than we can fathom (John 3:16), He stands solid on His commandments and promises to the point of eternal separation from those who do not [accept Him]. His majesty is beyond description, and when I stand before Him, although in respectful fear, I will feel His love and may someday have the courage to look up into His eyes."

Traditional Hindus believe that going against the Divine law will increase their karma, and thus delay their liberation, perhaps for hundreds of lifetimes. Becky knows the rules laid down by Roman Catholicism, and although she does not particularly like some of them—especially in her time of crisis—she is also fully aware of the judgment due her should she choose to do something else. She knows she is free to obey or disobey, and as such is a participant in the drama played out in her tradition after the fashion of Adam and Eve choosing to disobey God in the Garden of Eden.

Relationship with Divine

The cosmology of this system is hierarchical, with a clear delineation of authority in both heaven and earth. Every person in society has a proper place in this system, and life is easiest when roles are respected and embodied willingly. Family systems mirror the celestial hierarchy, with the father in charge, the mother obedient to him, and the children under the authority of both of them. Sam, a Southern Baptist deacon in Alaska, describes the relationship as being "very much like a father and child—love, faith, trust, and grace prevail."

The Divine is supremely beneficent and longs to enjoy relationship with every person. But the Divine also expects every creature to maintain its proper station. This can cause a great deal of ambivalence in believers, even the most devout. Asked to describe her relationship with the Divine, Ruth answered succinctly, "Quite literally love/hate." Yet others bear this ambivalence more easily, often as a result of hard losses. As Hal, an evangelical Christian, wrote, "After two quadruple by-pass surgeries and a light stroke, my walk is sweeter than ever. I have said many times, I wish I could have known him when I was young in the ministry with the abiding I have now—most of the time! I even pray for parking places now, and he usually gives them to me!"

Sherrie, a Conservative Jew in Miami, describes her relationship in a way that is distinctive to Traditional Judaism—as "one in which we both gain. I gain a spiritual elevation and peace of mind, and the Divine gains a partner in the ultimate redemption of the world."

Becky, in our case study, feels afraid to question God's law or His purpose—who is she to do so? She knows God loves her as a daughter, but a daughter is also expected to be submissive and obedient.

Meaning

In this system meaning is found by discerning the Divine will for one's life and aligning with that will to the greatest degree possible. As Sam wrote, "God's plan and will is perfect; however, ours is not. We have the freedom to choose activities contrary to God's intent. We choose alternatives that result in events and consequences that are not in accordance with his will. God, the Father, allows us to exercise our freedom of choice for a period but has always provided choices and alternatives that allow us to return to his plan. Many events that we perceive as 'bad' are merely the consequences of our free choice and selfish goals."

Traditional systems usually have a well-developed cosmology and eschatology, so believers have a good idea of what the Big Picture is, how they fit into it, and where everything is headed. Ruth, along with most Jews, sees the Divine will and human purpose aligned for an eschatological purpose, the "repair" of the cosmos: "The Torah . . . teaches that we all exist to heal and improve the world, the culmination of our efforts being the coming of *Moshiach* (Messiah)."

Ed's answer likewise focused on the eschatological dimension: "The world is doomed as the Bible foretold. We are now in the end times. The next Pope could very possibly become the Anti-Christ's right-hand man. The earth is telling us to beware of Christ's return soon, with threatening geological signs of all types from tsunami, earthquakes, erupting volcanos, droughts, loss of our atmospheric shelter, and melting ice caps to name a few. Cancer, AIDS, and deadly flu germs are another warning. All eyes must watch Israel, God's people, for the battle of all battles will be fought there."

Dharma, a devout Buddhist in Colorado, understands the "divine plan" as the movement of all beings toward Buddhahood, and sees meaning in putting the quest for liberation first in one's life. He writes, "My faith gives all the meaning in my life. Enlightenment is not just something that you achieve after a few years or lives, it is a quest that you must put first and foremost in your life in order to understand and achieve."

Becky, in our case study, has trouble reconciling the financial vicissitudes she and Tom are suffering with the demands of God's will. She knows she must submit, that she and Tom will do their duty, but she is scared and finds it difficult to trust that God will take care of them in the moment.

Diane serves her well by simply holding space for her to vent her feelings. Since Diane is also a Traditional Believer, she is not likely to try to change Becky's mind about anything. Even if Diane identified herself with another faith style, it would be unethical to try to convince Becky that something in her system is somehow "wrongheaded." Such spiritual arrogance has no place in spiritual guidance, and insight should be offered in ways congruent with the client's worldview.

Sources of Spiritual Wisdom

For most Traditional Believers, scripture and tradition are held in high esteem (even if not equal esteem, and even if other terms for these are used). For an evangelical Christian such as Ed, the answer is simple. He honors "the Holy Spirit and the Holy Bible," presumably in that order. Christine, writing from Anchorage, Alaska, communicates a profound certainty that is common to many Traditional Believers: "I know that the Holy Bible is divinely inspired and is the complete written word of God."

Many people who responded to the survey, however, did not find the sources of spiritual wisdom limited to these, but clearly identified scripture as the plumb line—the authority to which all other sources of wisdom must be subjected. As Sam described it, "My prayer is that I honor all sources of spiritual wisdom. I believe that the Bible is God's word and all other sources must be compared with it. God gave us the wisdom and understanding to discern his truth; however, we are sometimes influenced by many human factors and events. I believe that spiritual wisdom can sometimes be found in extremely illogical sources."

This generosity is echoed by Hal, who answered that his sources were "mostly, just biblical thought. But I believe truth is truth wherever you find it, and while the Bible is all true, all truth is not in the Bible. I use God's Word as my rule and guide for faith and practice. That doesn't mean I'm a Jerry Falwell religious politico, but that God's revelation is secure in my world."

For an Orthodox Jew, the Torah is the ultimate scriptural authority, but tradition as embodied in the Writings, the Prophets, the Talmud, and the synagogue rituals are also useful guides. Ruth adds more "human" sources to the list, honoring "Anyone who has in the past or is presently trying to live a life according to Torah from the Matriarchs to the Sages, Rebbeim, or the lovely old bubbe down the street."

Many sects will revere those sources common to their religion at large, but will also hold in equal esteem "proprietary" scriptures not honored by the larger tradition. For instance, amongst Christians, Seventh Day Adventists esteem not only the Bible, but also Ellen G. White's writings. Mormons add to the Bible the *Book of Mormon*, and Christian Scientists add Mary Baker Eddy's *Science and Health with Key to the Scriptures.*

Traditional Hindu Believers will likely all honor the Vedas and the Upanishads, but only some Shivite sects will esteem the *Shiva Purana*. Likewise, Buddhists are guided by both scripture and oral traditions, which will vary according to the specific school of Buddhism followed. Dharma's list included sources common to all Buddhists, but adds also those esteemed only by the Vajrayana school: "Buddha's teachings, the Dharma. The teachings of masters and Buddhas such as Lord Shakyamuni Buddha, Master Padmasambhava, His Holiness The Dalai Lama (all fourteen), etc."

For a Roman Catholic like Becky, in our case study, Diane will need to appeal to sources of wisdom honored by Becky's own system—to the Bible and to the teachings of the Roman Catholic Church—to assist her guidance. Likewise, anyone who companions a Traditional Believer must be careful to appeal only to those the client him- or herself believes to be authoritative. Any other wisdom sources may be helpful for insight or comparison, but must at least conform to the authority found in those accepted sources.

Spiritual Growth

Traditional Believers are likely to evaluate Spiritual Growth by the extent to which one has submitted one's own will to the Divine will, and surrendered one's own understanding to the external authority of scripture and tradition. Failure to submit or surrender is seen as rebelliousness, which is inherently sinful. "Islam" is the Arabic word for "submission," and the struggle required to submit one's own will to that of Allah is what is meant by *jihad*—not holy war as we have been misled by extremists to believe, but an internal battle fought by each believer to achieve holiness. As Ruth wrote, she measures her own growth "by the capacity I have to do *mitzvahs* [good deeds or holy duties] and stop myself from doing *aveiros* [harmful or evil deeds]. On another level, by how much I allow things that have no worth to distract me from those things."

Respondents were quick to point out that this is often a long and arduous process. Dharma writes, "Spiritual growth is only something that you achieve through lives and lives of training and meditation. You must understand in order to achieve, and you must achieve in order to understand."

Though he would not agree that it takes many lives, Ed was likewise focused on the long-term process of spiritual growth when he wrote: "It's a day-by-day walk with the Lord. Speaking to him, and seeking his reply through prayer, the Word, and fellowship with brethren. We have to realize we are not perfect, and never will be while on earth. But we must keep trying."

Nick agrees, and adds that the evidence for such growth is manifest in our behavior: "Spiritual growth is sometimes slow, but it is guided by God through his Holy Word. When we accept Christ as our Savior, we begin to look at life differently. The more God lives in us, the more mature we become. We can measure this maturity by our walk with God. Our maturity is manifest through our love for God and others, our willingness to live for God, our charity, hope, and peace."

Practices

Among all the respondents, the number one practice for Traditional Believers is prayer (or, in some traditions, meditation). The sincerity of Ed's emotion is clear when he speaks about what prayer means to him: "To be able to speak to the Creator of the Universe and have him listen, without being shot with a bolt of lightning, is awesome."

Dharma describes a Buddhist perspective when he says his chief practices include: "Meditation—without it, we would have no insight. Prayer, because we must worship and pay homage to the buddhas and bodhisattvas in order to attain enlightenment and have guidance."

The second most common response was reading scripture. Ed wrote that scripture contains God's "words of direction that were [written] through men and women he chose that were filled with his Holy Spirit. There is nothing that the Bible doesn't have an answer to. The basics of men and women never change. We've had the same needs since time began, so the Bible never becomes obsolete or outdated. Simply quoting a scripture can give one the strength to move mountains, let alone make it through the day."

Many people also mentioned worship, especially the corporate variety, which includes prayer, ritual, and song. Dharma said, "Worship is extremely important, because you can purify your karma and help other sentient beings through worship of the buddhas and bodhisattvas." Ed writes, "There are more songs about Jesus than any other human ever on earth. That alone says something."

Only one person each mentioned studying nature or activism as practices important to them. While most Traditional Believers might agree that these are important, most would agree with Sam that "meditation, nature, and activism . . . have value; however, they would be secondary to worship, prayer, and scripture."

Advantages

The Traditional Believer's paradigm is certainly attractive. The orderly hierarchy imposed upon the chaos of creation and the clearly stated moral requirements of the Traditional model afford believers a great rock of safety in what otherwise often feels like a very scary world.

Ed is passionate as he describes this sense of safety: "The Creator of the universe loves *me*. I will never loose my salvation. God is always with me, no matter where I am. When I do sin, after asking his forgiveness, his unlimited grace will forgive me, and he will remove my transgressions, as far as the east is from the west (Ps 103:12). He has a perfect plan for me and my life and will provide for my every need. I'm told to never worry, because he knows the number of hairs on my head (Matt 10:30), who I was before time began, and would have died for me alone. I know that I'm not an accident. Through

Christ I can defeat the enemy. After I die on earth, I'll be raised with resurrection power to serve him enthusiastically and continually (Rev 7:15) in unimaginable ways."

Hal concurs with this view, adding that the advantages to his faith include "peace, assurance of salvation, and a fellowship with Jesus Christ through his Holy Spirit for daily needs and not just a 'crisis Christ' when I need something. He answers prayer and has preserved me and my wife in [dire] circumstances. . . . I can trust in something unshakable in a world that seems to be running headlong into Hell."

Dharma is likewise secure in his belief that he is making progress toward spiritual liberation: "I believe in my faith, so I believe that I am preventing births in lower realms, etc., and further achieving my goal of enlightenment."

Believers feel secure in that they stand fast in a system that has stood the test of time, which, depending on the tradition, may have provided safety for the faithful for thousands of years. As Sherrie says of her Judaism, "It encompasses all aspects of life—very few contradictions. [It is] time tested."

Disadvantages

There are also dangers to the Traditional paradigm that even those who live within this system acknowledge and must therefore exercise caution. Hal mentions the "danger of being too narrow and too conservative. I can't embrace comparative religions for I don't believe that there is any other path to God except through his son, Jesus. It is a careful walk not to become judgmental of others who do not know my Lord, or embrace his truth."

Traditional Believers may also confuse the hierarchical authority of the Divine for the authority of a religious hierarchy, or even a local community leader. Though one may trust the Divine to be just, human representatives of the Divine have a less than stellar record. Sam acknowledges this danger, but is ultimately hopeful about it: "God has chosen to work through us in this world, and due to our freedom of choice, many of us fail to achieve the potential he provides. God's will shall prevail; however, our failure to adhere to God's will and achieve our potential requires time-consuming alternatives and unwanted consequences."

Blind obedience to hierarchical authority has resulted in some of the world's greatest evils, and it is hard to see how the Divine might have actually willed some of them (such as the crusades, the Jonestown massacre, or the genocide in Rwanda). Traditional Believers may also need to be reminded at times of the balance between Divine judgment and mercy. Jesus may have said, "If thine eye offend thee pluck it out," (Matthew 18:9) but few spiritual guides (even those operating from within the Traditional paradigm) would have counseled Origen to castrate himself. Spiritual guides may need to remind Traditional Believers that the Divine mercy is often more generous than our own proclivity for self-condemnation may suggest.

Some respondents indicated that the biggest disadvantage was prejudice toward their faith. Hal names "the current backlash in the liberal media against anything that smacks of this personal encounter with God, but how can they know when they don't know Jesus?"

Conclusion of Case

After more discussion of Becky's feelings, it is the security of God's sovereignty to which Diane appeals in her guidance. "Becky, do you think God makes mistakes?"

"No . . . no, of course not."

"So, if you are pregnant, will that be a mistake on God's part?"

"No, it can't be."

"I don't think so, either. I also don't think it's a punishment. God does not punish with blessings. The Church teaches us that children are always blessings, and God does not bestow them as a judgment. God just doesn't work that way."

"I know that . . . I want to trust that. I just don't know how we're going to stretch our budget any further."

"Becky, the Bible says that 'God owns the cattle on a thousand hills.' 'The earth is the Lord's and all that is within it.' If all the riches in heaven and earth are God's, don't you think He is going to provide you with what you need?"

Becky nodded.

Diane pulled her Bible off the shelf and opened it. "I'm going to read you some scripture, and I want to invite you to imagine that this is Jesus himself talking just to you. Can you do that?" Becky nodded again and closed her eyes, as Diane read from the twelfth chapter of Luke.

"Jesus is saying to you, 'Do not worry about your life, what you will eat or what you will drink, or about your body, what you will wear. Is not life more than food, and the body more than clothing? Look at the birds of the air; they neither sow nor reap nor gather into barns, and yet your heavenly Father feeds them. Are you not of more value than they? And can any of you by worrying add a single hour to your span of life? . . . So do not worry about tomorrow, for tomorrow will bring worries of its own. Today's trouble is enough for today.'" Diane sat in silence for a while. "Were you able to hear Jesus speaking to you?"

"Yes, it was wonderful. I just need to let go of my fear and give this whole thing to God. If I can be faithful to God, I know God will be faithful to me."

Guiding Traditional Believers requires upholding the Traditional paradigm, keeping doubt and discouragement at bay, and supporting clients as they find their place in the divine hierarchy. The Traditional worldview is, more than any other style, a place of safety and security, and clients will be well served when they can learn to rest in this security. The Divine is fully in charge, and as dark as things may seem to us, in the long view all is as it should be, and all will end in glory. The Traditional Believer stakes a claim in this glory and devotes his or her life to serving the Divine as its purpose is worked out.

This style is by far the most common and is similar to Fowler's "Synthetic-Conventional" stage, Peck's "Formal-Institutional" stage, and Schwing's "The Theist" orientation.

Traditional Believers At-a-Glance

1. *How is the Divine imaged?* As sovereign of the universe.
2. *What is the nature of one's relationship with the Divine?* Hierarchical, as a child in the divine family.
3. *How does one construct meaning in the world?* By discerning and acting out the divine will.
4. *What are the accepted sources of spiritual wisdom?* Scripture and tradition.
5. *How is spiritual growth assessed?* The extent to which one submits one's own will to the Divine's.

6. *Practices honored?* Prayer, studying scripture, corporate worship.
7. *Advantages?* Security and clear answers.
8. *Disadvantages?* Rigidity, spiritual arrogance, and blind obedience.

2

Spiritual Eclectics

Maya phoned her spiritual guide late at night, depressed and frustrated. Mike asked her to come by his office first thing in the morning, and he arrived early to make sure there was hot tea waiting for her when she got there. Maya was a few minutes late, as usual, and she sunk into her chair with a palpable heaviness. "Thanks for seeing me on short notice. It's not like it's an emergency or anything."

"I'm just glad I had the time open." Mike sat down and lit a candle. "This is to remind us there are three—" just then Mike's dog walked into the room, "—four of us here." Mike smiled at Maya and patted his dog on the head. "Tell me what's happening."

Maya was a regular at Spirit Rock, a Buddhist retreat center that practices Vipassana, or insight meditation. She had a special devotion to Kali, a Hindu goddess of fierce aspect, and also to the Virgin Mary. Images of both adorned her bedroom altar, as well as her keychain. She also occasionally attended a Jewish Renewal synagogue with friends.

"I feel empty," Maya started. "Do you remember how, about two months ago, I was feeling this great spiritual rush? It was like the world was alive with Spirit. Spirit was everywhere, I could feel it when I breathed." She captured a bit of the energy of that memory . . . then her head slunk down again. "Where did Spirit go, Mike?"

"What makes you think Spirit has gone anywhere?"

"I can't seem to access it. Everything seems so . . . mundane. I try to meditate, and I feel like I have nothing but sawdust in my chest. In fact, I can't meditate. I feel like someone just opened a big window in the sky and all that was ever spiritual or holy just got sucked out of the world." She paused for a moment. "I feel abandoned."

"Do you think Spirit has really abandoned you?"

"No, it can't have. It just *feels* like it. As long as the universe is here, Spirit is here—but for some reason I'm just not able to see it right now. And it's painful. It feels empty and alone."

Much of Maya's distress is related to the dissonance between what she believes and how she feels—something all of our clients must deal with at some time or another. For Maya it was doubly perplexing because it was only a few weeks ago that she felt the Divine in a very animated way in her life. She was not ready for such a deep valley so soon after experiencing the height of spiritual ecstasy.

Spiritual Eclectics like Maya are those who have a very active spiritual life, but do not adhere to any one faith tradition. Allergic to dogmatic approaches to faith, Eclectics approach their spirituality buffet-style: a little of this, a little of that. They might hold an image of a loving creator left over from Sunday school, accept a largely Hindu cosmology (including karma and reincarnation), and practice a Buddhist form of meditation, or any other conceivable combination. They also make up a significant proportion of the population; according to a 2001 Gallup Poll, 33 percent of Americans describe themselves as "spiritual but not religious." This style is original to Schwing's system, and his name for the orientation is adopted here as well.

Divine Image

Spiritual Eclectics are most likely to be pantheists (the Divine and the universe are identical), to view all things as One, and themselves as part of that One. Though they may be a small part, they nonetheless also see themselves as identified with the whole. As Lisa from southeastern U.S. put it, "I do not envision a personalized God. I see the Divine as everywhere and in all. . . . Like an ocean of consciousness . . . an eternal, omnipresent force that underlies all."

Kevin, an Episcopal priest from California, agrees, saying, "There is only one Everything, and I am part of it. The Mystery of existence is an ecstatic joy for me. Tao pervades all."

The Hindu motto found in the Upanishads, "Thou art that," describes well the Eclectic perspective. An Eclectic might say, "This house is me, that dog is me, you are me, the Horsehead Nebula is me. Since the Divine is all things, including me, I also coinhere in all things, and *am* all things." Thomas, a ministerial student in California, describes the experience of this unity: "I feel . . . the divine presence within me and surrounding me. I behold God within and without; this is my single-pointed contemplation. That said, living into this full presence is an excruciating joy, my perception/illusion often falls far short of this realization, yet I can understand the universe in no other manner."

Since the Divine is in everything, anything can be used as a locus of one's worship and attention. Spiritual Eclectics often construct altars in their homes (sometimes many of them), and it is fascinating to see what images appear there. (Asking Spiritual Eclectics what is on their altars this week is a wonderful way to kick off a guidance session.) I have seen altars with such varied representations of Divinity as icons of the Blessed Virgin, pictures of various saints, statues of Shiva or Ganesha, drawings by three-year-olds, photos of dogs and cats, figurines of ancient goddesses, and an action figure of Homer Simpson. Eclectics construct their own pantheons made up of images that resonate with them, sometimes for reasons unknown to them, but intuitively important.

As Wiccan hospital chaplain Terry writes, "My primary image of the Divine is a three-fold person of Nymph, Mother, and Crone. She is friend, lover, mother, Goddess; she is the ever-young, beautiful, pointy-eared queen of the faery; she is Divine Mother. The Divine also manifests to me as the God. He is strong, gentle, protective, loving, wild, and sexual. He is hairy; he has horns and is goat-hooved.

"The Divine manifests to me as my line of gurus: Jesus Christ, Babaji-Krishna, Lahiri Mahasaya, Swami Sri Yukteswar, and Paramahansa Yogananda."

Seminary instructor Renee sums up the Eclectic approach to the divine image eloquently when she writes, "The Divine is everywhere and assumes and/or works through persona, metaphors, creatures, visages, the arts, beauty, suffering, all that assists me in knowing the ultimate truth of Oneness. At different times in my life different images instruct me, lead me, entice me, lure me toward the Great Mystery of Love and Union; the constant is the drawing toward, the inviting beyond where I am, the longing to incarnate, to make tangible that Oneness, that Love. Presently the Divine comes to me as the Lover and the Beloved."

Relationship with Divine

Since Spiritual Eclectics view all things as part of the Divine, including themselves, relationship with the Divine is a form of self-knowledge. To know Divinity is to truly know oneself (and vice versa). For some eclectics, such as Burton, this results in a relationship of often astounding intimacy: "I would describe it as both intimate and inescapable. By intimate I mean that it pursues every level of life, from how I feel and get along in the world at large, to my most personal thoughts and reflections. It is not afar off, somewhere else, like 'heaven,' nor is it some-when else, as in a future event or 'coming kingdom.' It is always here and always now. By inescapable I mean that the Divine seeps into every crevice continually, relentlessly."

For Renee, this intimacy permeates every aspect of life: "The Divine has had a hold on me from my very beginnings. I belong to the Divine. The images have changed, but the hold never has. It is that searing, branding, or chemical bonding that happens when supposedly two entities recognize each other as one. My total humanity is involved: the range of emotions and the various transitions I experience are part of this unique relationship as well. Therefore, there are times of great struggle, overwhelming fear, misdirected anger, profound disappointment, deep peace, immense joy, a dynamic hope, and tender love . . . and did I mention laughter and delight? Yes, of course."

For many, this intimacy takes on a sexual quality. As Terry relates, "The Divine is lover, friend, mother, Beloved Goddess, and the deepest part of me and everyone else." Yet, in spite of this aspect of love mysticism, this intimacy is not always without ambivalence. Kevin experiences the interplay between "Tao, who is my lover, and my own varying degrees of awareness. I embrace the Dark Side of the Mystery along with the Light. If you think that is scary, how do you think Tao feels?"

For some eclectics, this experience of intimacy can be frustratingly intermittent. Nate, a ceremonial magician, relates that his relationship with Divinity is constantly "flickering in and out of intimacy—sometimes in for days, sometimes out for months."

Lisa elaborates on this inconsistent intimacy: "My relationship to the Divine is undisciplined, yet frequent touchpoints do occur that make me feel connected within to the Divine-That-Is-Within-All. I experience the Divine as being within me; sometimes I am more aware of this reality than others. At times (not infrequently), I feel like a sail that is filled with the Divine wind, sailing forth in joy. At other times the Divine feels like a buried treasure that I can't quite see underneath the mud. (On some occasions the whole aspect of Divinity feels remote and theoretical, but at such times, I draw on the weight of my own and others' experiences that the Divine is real—more real, in fact, than what we call the 'real world,' and subsequently I find the cloud of 'unknowing' dissipates, like a passing mood.)"

C. K. represents the other end of the spectrum, as his experience is almost completely void of intimacy, which only emphasizes the diverse nature of Spiritual Eclectics' experience. He describes his relationship with the Divine as "passive at best. I consider myself a tiny component in an incomprehensibly large process, a bit of flotsam being carried along by an enormous wave started eons ago. I talk to the creator, but feel I am largely talking to myself, looking for perspective. I'd like to think that there are more direct channels of interaction with god, but have never found one—at least from *here*, and I have to think that there is a reason for that, that it's part of the design."

Eclectics may use many words for the Divine, depending upon mood or circumstance. They may have one name for the Divine when it is experienced as an external reality (Brahma, God, Jesus, Allah, the Goddess), and another name for the Divine as experienced internally (Atman, Spirit, the Inner Light, Divine Spark), and still other names for particular manifestations in specific contexts. If directing an Eclectic, it will be handy to keep a tally of such names so that one can use the right one depending on the context of the discussion. Regardless of what name is used, Eclectics never lose sight of being a part of the reality being named, and they are very aware of a responsibility to increase their conscious participation in the life of the Divine and will work to promote increased consciousness in their culture.

Meaning

Spiritual Eclectics owe much of their spiritual path to the countercultural trailblazers of the sixties, otherwise known as the "hippies." The sixties youth culture really inaugurated the eclectic impulse in contemporary spirituality by mixing elements from Western and Eastern religious traditions, but also by incorporating many beliefs and practices from native sources. Whereas previous generations were likely to see such disciplines as astrology and Tarot reading as demonic, Spiritual Eclectics have embraced both the goodness of Divinity and the usefulness of divination without any apparent contradiction. They are likely to perceive such prohibitions as closed-minded and spiritually prejudiced.

Owing as much as they do to the hippie culture, it is no surprise that many of the issues that invigorated that movement still carry great charge for Eclectics. They are very likely to be concerned about the environment, gender equality (including equality for sexual minorities), and peace and justice issues. These are not just ideological artifacts likely to fade as the connection to sixties counterculture becomes more tenuous, but are in many ways intrinsic to the Eclectic worldview. Eclectics have no generally accepted view of the afterlife (views on this, like everything else, are eclectic), but most would agree that all life is sacred, and this planet is the only place where we know life exists in the universe. It is therefore our sacred duty to protect and preserve the earth for succeeding generations. As Edward from Texas relates, meaning for him is found "through service to my fellow man, and action to make our world a better place. I find meaning in my own existence, and knowing that, as there is a divine spark in you, there is also one in me."

This is a sort of nature mysticism (since everything is Divine, and the earth, too, may be perceived as a goddess) that provides primary meaning for Eclectics. Renee expands upon this kind of mysticism: "Since I can remember, meaning in life has come from being of service to another. Consequently, I have given my entire life to service. However, for too many reasons to address here, I am more and more convinced that I must come to accept myself, the Divine, all persons, and, indeed, all creatures, animate and inanimate, as having meaning just because we exist. It is too long into the evolution of creation to purport that we, or life, are only meaningful if we are utilitarian. I am reminded of Abraham Heschel's inspiration, 'Just to be is a blessing, just to live is holy.'"

There is a slight sense of danger in this worldview. Even though everything is Divine, greater awareness (self-awareness, if you will) of the Divine is of paramount importance for Divinity's own self-fulfillment. The evolution of self-reflexive humans is a great achievement in this project of Divine self-awareness. Without bending to anthropocentric self-importance, Eclectics value the human capacity for consciousness and see it as something to be protected and promoted. If we blew ourselves up in a great atomic cloud, it would not only be a great sin against Life (so many plants and animals would die), but it would also be a great setback in Divine self-awareness if humans were to be wiped out. Preserving and increasing consciousness is therefore one of the chief ways Eclectics find meaning.

As Ursula relates, such an orientation brings with it a great deal of responsibility: "The divine experiences I have had have taught me a lot about the universal connection everything has with each other, from people to cats to rocks to clouds to parasites. Sometimes I can see the Divine in the rotting animal carcass on the side of the road. In rare moments I can see the Divine in the raving lunatic in the street.... Everything happens for reasons that we can't ever understand. And our actions create ripples that go on and on and on for more years than we can comprehend."

Sources of Spiritual Wisdom

Spiritual eclectics assume that all religions point toward the Truth, but that no particular path *is* the Truth. As Edward writes, "I honor all faiths, for all have something valuable to teach us. Each perceives a part or aspect of the infinite Divine. As God is not contained in one book, he is also too large to be contained in all of them combined . . . but each sees a part of him. I also honor the thoughts of other religious seekers, for they also have a part of the Divine within them. As such, my faith demands I respect all faiths willing to respect me."

But Eclectics do not insist that spiritual wisdom comes from traditional religious sources. As Frog says, "You never know when and whence wisdom will suddenly appear. You never know when and where wisdom will slowly take shape. It could come from anywhere or anyone. It could be triggered by anything." C. K. prefers scientific sources to traditional spiritual ones. He honors "nature and science, especially physics. I call science 'that small portion of the language of God that we have learned to speak ourselves.' I believe that all the important principles we need to be aware of are woven throughout the whole of creation, obvious for any who care to look. I reject most of the 'traditional' sources of wisdom, the ones that come from mankind, as I believe they are completely flawed by hidden motives such as greed, power, or lust."

Most Eclectics would agree with C. K. that all religious traditions err and so should be held lightly. As Renee relates, "I want to think that I honor all sources of wisdom. Then I start cogitating, 'Wisdom is relative.' I believe I am respectful, which is different than honoring, of many different sources of spiritual wisdom. The ones I honor are the ones that feed, nourish, encourage, and support me on my inner journey. These sources include an introduction to quantum physics, a novel by a contemporary writer, poetry, a movie, children, any of the great mystics, nature . . . the sources are endless."

Thus, among Eclectics there is often great esteem for established faith traditions, but also a distrust of any spiritual authority put forward by them. Eclectics have internalized a postmodern view that wisdom is subjective, and that everyone must find out what is true for him- or herself, that there is no one path to enlightenment or salvation (however such terms might be understood by the individual). Marmot, from Illinois, says that the sources of spiritual wisdom she honors are "any that I can get my hands on and my heart into."

Eclectics, true to their name, pick and choose elements of various faith traditions that are useful to them in the moment. They will pick up wisdom from various scriptures, teachers, liturgies, even popular culture in their neverending quest for Truth, but they will also just as quickly set any of these aside when they encounter another bit of wisdom that makes more sense in the moment. Goku's sources of wisdom are often in flux, but he reports, "Right now, it's Buddhism and Taoism. I may change over time, but I do try to use two at all times."

Goku's limiting himself to two spiritual sources is unusual for Eclectics. Much more indicative is Terry's smorgasbord of spiritual authorities: "My spirituality is informed by the *Tao Te Ching*, and the *Bhavagad Gita*, as well as the writings of the Sufi and Christian mystics. I honor the teachings of my gurus, especially Jesus Christ and Paramahansa Yogananda, as well as the Pagan and Western Mystery traditions of the West. I practice Theravada Buddhism, based on the earliest Buddhist scriptures."

Nate's list of accepted authorities is even more comprehensive: "Zoroaster, Siddharta Gautama, Lao-tsu, Pythagoras, Orpheus, Parmenides, Empedocles, Socrates, Plato, Plotinus, the *Corpus Hermeticum*, Zosimos, Valentinus, the Barbelo Gnostics, *Thunder, Perfect Mind*, Iamblicus, Proclus, *Sefer Yetzirah*, Mohammed (to a degree), Dhul Nun al-Misri, Hallaj, the Ikhwan al-Safa, the Sabians of Harran, Jafar al-Siddiq, Hassan i Sabbah, Suhrawardi al-Maqtul, Ibn Arabi, Garab Dorje, Padmasambhava, Machig Labdron, Sankara, Ramon Llull, Cusanus, Paracelsus, Ficino, John Dee, Shakespeare, Johann Andraea, Thomas Taylor, William Blake, Emerson, William James, Whitehead, Bohm, Gurdjieff, Krishnamurti, Steiner, Dmitri Mitrinovic, Hazrat Inayat Khan, Murshid Sam Lewis, Pir Vilayat Khan, Gregory Bateson, Paolo Soleri, Idries Shah, Henry Corbin, Stafford Beer, Buckminster Fuller, Oscar Ichazo, Tarthang Tulku, E. J. Gold, Mike Oldfield, Kate Bush, Robert Fripp, Nema, Alan Moore, Maturana and Varela, Rowena Pattee Kryder, Sam Webster, Namkhai Norbu, Eckhart Tolle, Integral Transformative Practice, Peter Kingsley, A. H. Almaas, Van Nguyen, Saniel Bonder, and Linda Groves-Bonder, among others."

Unlike Traditional Believers, for whom all spiritual authority is external, Spiritual Eclectics tend to view the opposite as true. External authorities for them are all suspect (though oftentimes very useful), but the supreme authority is internal. Only the Spiritual Eclectic gets to say what is true for him or her, and very often one's own body is a valued source of wisdom.

Spiritual Growth

Highly influenced by Eastern traditions, the spiritual process for the Eclectic is often to see through the illusion of separateness, to realize the essential Oneness of all things. The ability to experience this unity usually brings with it a host of positive traits. As Burton describes it, we recognize that growth has occurred "when we find ourselves freer to be more loving and less demanding, more embracing and less discriminating, more mindful of the present and less abstracted into past or future—more unitive and less divisive." Terry agrees, adding, "Spiritual growth is evidenced by increasing love, compassion, joy, equanimity, happiness, and the experience of divine union."

Contemplative practices like meditation and mindfulness are helpful in reaching this goal, but many other modalities, such as breathwork, bodywork, psychedelics, and sex are also useful tools when used consciously and in a proper, sacred container. Renee expands on this list: "The process may include excerpts from scriptures, wisdom literature, visual art, music, movement, story-telling, prose, poetry, theater, cinema, and/or journaling; whatever helps the person articulate her/his story and come to insight and integration."

Spiritual Eclectics find meaning in the emotional experience of oneness and will pursue almost any means that might facilitate such a sensation. Thus, Maya's experience in our case study seems almost overwhelming since, despite her hard work, the felt experience of unity with Spirit is evading her.

For many Eclectics, growth can be understood in terms of fulfilling one's innate potential. Edward says he understands spiritual growth as "becoming all you are capable of being. Being is the gift given to us by God, and you grow spiritually by living fully, loving wastefully, and being all that one can be."

This fulfillment of human potential necessarily includes the ability to integrate painful and even negative experiences. Renee describes it in a metaphor drawn from the Christian tradition: "I . . . believe that the depth of one's self-knowledge, awareness, and integrity, the motivation and quality of one's actions, the congruence between the inner and outer life, and the experience of living through suffering and how one has navigated it—Christians call it the Paschal Mystery, nature affords this same metaphor of dying and rising to new life—give insight into a person's spiritual . . . maturity."

Ursula calls this a facility for transformation: "I interpret spiritual growth in myself and others when I see transformation. I really see spiritual growth as a willingness to let parts of ourselves die so that others may be reborn. I admire those that can face their shadows and learn from them. I see spiritual growth in people who can let go of old patterns and ways of being and transform their lives, even when it means leaving behind friends and family."

For many Eclectics, one part that must die in order to be transformed is the ego, the part of ourselves that likes to think it is separate and in control—for it must be shown to be a fraud. Head knowledge of this masquerade is an important first step, but an experiential knowledge of unity and the eradication of the ego is a cherished goal of spiritual growth for Eclectics. Theo recognizes progress "in my ability and willingness to skillfully grow from those moments when I act out of my own illusionary concepts or egotistical beliefs (self separation from the Divine) that I know preclude me from listening/acting compassionately or reflecting clearly."

Practices

The practices honored by Spiritual Eclectics are as varied as their sources of wisdom. Marmot notes that these are rarely static: "The matter of spiritual practices is ever-evolving. If one is interfaith, there are many choices to be made and constant adjustments for a harmonious combination."

Practices most often mentioned by Eclectics include prayer, meditation, and ritual, and often all three. Kevin describes his daily morning discipline thusly: "Get up, get dressed, eat breakfast, and then go into my study and close the door. I allow my Japanese meditation bowl to sound. I chant one of the [poems from the] *Tao Te Ching*, using plainsong. I often like to chant one of the *Odes of Solomon*." Lisa notes that she practices "a variety of types of meditation, depending on how the Spirit moves at any given time."

Eclectics also enjoy sacred readings from the scriptures of various traditions, as well as from the writings of mystics, poets, philosophers, artists, and scientists. Divination and dreamwork are also popular practices.

Philosophical inquiry was also frequently mentioned by the respondents. Lisa describes her practice as "contemplating the transience of earthly life and keeping aware of the inevitability of death (death as my advisor, in the vein of Carlos Castaneda)."

Eclectics are very embodied in their spiritual practice on the whole. Arts and crafts are a common feature of Eclectic practice, as are disciplines such as writing poetry and journaling. Exercise, especially yoga and Tai Chi, are also prominent. Kevin wrote, "My daily practice now includes a half hour to an hour of biking or walking out to the Baylands Park created out of a former garbage dump (great transformational symbolism there!)."

This embodied spirituality leads many to seek inspiration from being in nature and an attention to nature's cycles. Lisa especially values being in the "mountains or by a rushing stream (definitely high up there in importance)—and envisioning the stream flowing through me." Thomas doesn't have to go far to connect this way with the natural world. One of his favorite practices is "working in the garden . . . [or] taking a hike in the wilderness. I find there is usually an opening into a sacred space wherever I am."

Consistent with their concern for social justice, spiritual practice for Eclectics usually includes some form of activism or service. Lisa seeks to be "open to divine marching orders in my social change work and feeling the energy working in me to accomplish valuable actions. [I value] being with people in a way that eases their distress—being of service to people on a psychological/spiritual level."

Just as the deities honored by Eclectics may be all over the map, those following this style are likewise varied in the environments in which they seek to worship. Marmot lists a few of her favorites: "Catholic, Orthodox, Quaker, Bahai, Islamic, Buddhist, Jewish, Zoroastrian, Jain, Hindu, Pagan in my metro area."

Spiritual Eclectics honor a greater variety of spiritual practices than any other style—perhaps more than all the other styles put together. For this reason, those guiding Eclectics should feel free to suggest practices from wildly disparate sources. Since for Eclectics everything is sacred, practices will either be "helpful" or "unhelpful" rather than "right" or "wrong." They will decide if a practice is right "for them" at this time, holding open the possibility that a practice might gain meaning in the future even if it holds limited appeal in the present. Directors should not be shy about this: Spiritual Eclectics are often eager to try new practices—they might discard them shortly, but may indeed find meaning in them for a time, often great meaning.

Spiritual discipline is not usually high on the Eclectics' list of honored virtues, but often there will be a handful of practices that will have enduring value for Eclectics that will ground them, even as they continue to experiment with others.

Advantages

There are many attractive elements to the Spiritually Eclectic path. Those who walk it are predisposed to have great respect for people of every faith tradition, and therefore have access to a wide variety of images and practices. Terry writes, "My kind of faith . . . embraces spiritual wisdom from many sources and so provides many tools and opportunities to explore the depths of ourselves and our relationship to the Divine." Edward concurs, adding that an eclectic faith offers "a greater tolerance and acceptance in a world where such are becoming more and more rare. I am not locked into any particular dogmatic creed, and can freely learn from all of human thought and religious wisdom. My faith is mine, for I had a hand in deciding what resonates with me. Also, by recognizing the Divine in all life, you begin to gain a different perspective on mankind's place in the world, his future, and his responsibility for his own beliefs."

Eclectics generally see their distance from organized religion as a good thing, as so many have experienced spiritual abuse in their communities of origin. As C. K. told me, as a Spiritual Eclectic, "it is impossible for someone else to take advantage of my beliefs, to use them to manipulate me for personal gain, as I believe is at the core of nearly all organized religions. There's no authority figure, no book of rules to follow, no punishments for disobedience, no calls to kill—or even disenfranchise—the infidels."

Eclectics can worship and celebrate in almost any spiritual context without feeling insincere or out of place, which affords them an almost radical spiritual generosity. Theo told me, "I believe that my spiritual experience has enabled me to truly feel the presence of Spirit in every moment; to respect and reflect the divine Spirit for others; to respect, see, and honor the presence of Spirit of all faith traditions; to experience Spirit on a very personal basis; to care deeply about the spirit path of all beings, remaining absolutely committed to deepen these paths in any way that I am able; to realize that every being is on a path toward God/Spirit and to be committed to the progress on our full realization of the presence of Spirit. I believe that ultimately all paths of Spirit meet at the heart and this allows me to move toward and embody the Spirit that is the essence of all faiths."

Eclectics can also tolerate great ambiguity in both their inner and outer worlds without disorientation, and find themselves on equal footing with a wide variety of people, a position of both humility and strength. As Marmot writes, "Since I honor all paths, have some information about many of them, and take a 'not instead-of but in-addition-to' stance, I can honor everyone, including people who say they don't believe in anything. (What does 'believe in' mean, anyway?) This stance renders me always eager to learn from/about others—a lens and focus for mental and physical travel."

Another advantage of such openness to the wide diversity of faiths is that one's spiritual journey almost never gets boring. There are always new practices to attempt, new perspectives to explore, new beliefs to "try on for size." This almost eliminates the spiritual stagnation that can occur when one is immersed for a long time within one tradition. As Lisa describes it, "To have important points of contact with numerous faith traditions makes me all the more in touch with the fact that there are 'many wells but One Source.' That is to say, there isn't much chance of me getting stuck and mired within one way of seeing things, because my path has so many different strands and is inclusive by its very nature. I have many potential points of contact to people and their beliefs. To me, this is the only way I could possibly go about it. To be locked into one set of beliefs as 'the way' feels dishonest to the reality of the breadth of the Divine and the multiplicity of paths to the Summit. Also, I think my path has encouraged an autonomous, independent growth-seeking in myself, which hasn't been dependent on the reinforcement and example of others. I've forged my own path, and this has made for a deeper, richer journey."

Spiritual Eclectics feel and promote respect for those who are different from them, and are great advocates for the welfare of the poor, racial and sexual minorities, human and animal rights, as well as the preservation of the planet. Spiritual Eclectics are responsible for much cultural and political progress in the past thirty-five years, and will be very important indeed in forming the social agenda of the coming generation.

Disadvantages

The downside of the Spiritually Eclectic journey is that since all paths are honored, there is sometimes insufficient discernment applied to new sources of spiritual wisdom. Cults and abusive gurus often find willing prey among Eclectics, and often new revelations are given equal weight to those that have stood the test of time.

But for those who have been able to steer clear of charlatans and abusive leaders, a prominent complaint involves identity issues and the lack of a supportive spiritual community in which to practice. As Renee writes,

Eclectics "have little sense, if any, of a home base or a place in community where s/he could be supported, challenged, formed, and honed. A person could just wander aimlessly from one experience to another, never integrating the experiences or being transformed by them."

Lisa agrees, noting the difficulties of a solitary path are often internal: "Not being anchored in a particular faith community with particular rules and traditions, I sometimes have had self-doubts to conquer. I've had to ensure my own inner coordinates for the path are solid. Ultimately this is an advantage, but when I'm in a more tentative place with myself about this self-hewn path, it can feel like a disadvantage in the moment."

Hand in hand with the lack of community is the lack of spiritual accountability. Spiritual directors can help Eclectics by providing such accountability, by holding up the mirror of their own stated values to see if their actions are congruent with them.

Another disadvantage is that it is frightfully difficult at times to explain exactly where one is coming from, spiritually, especially to people not of this faith style. As Theo describes it, "Due to its highly personal nature, it may be difficult to express the nature of my spirit belief so that others can understand or relate to it. Sometimes it is easiest to say I am a Buddhist—that of course is only a partial truth. My approach to Spirit may be perceived to be slightly out of the mainstream, which means that the mainstream may have difficulty in ascribing credibility to my eclectic approach."

Terry agrees, a note of frustration creeping into his responses, "People tend to want easy-to-understand answers to what my religion is, and there is no simple answer. Also, there are paradoxes inherent in a broad experience of how the Divine manifests, and these apparent conflicts can be challenging."

Lisa adds, wistfully, "I long for the simple, straightforward sort of path that is easy to explain without raising eyebrows and provoking mystification on the part of more traditional folks who don't understand why someone would want such a multi-faceted path."

There can also be a lack of groundedness amongst Eclectics. Since there is no "right way" to follow this path, many are blown hither and thither by every new teacher or spiritual fad without ever setting down roots in a spiritual tradition. As Goku writes, there is "no set of rituals, ceremonies, and no true religious history that is rich as others like Buddhism and Islam, and no religious library other than the Universe itself."

Because of this, there is a great lack of appropriate direction and accountability, which is where spiritual guidance can be very helpful indeed to Eclectics. The "self-starter" nature of the style is difficult for many. As C. K. wrote, "It's not *easy*. Everything is all up to the individual. When I feel lost, there is no one to turn to, no guidebook to show me the way. I don't believe any other religion provides that either, but they at least offer the *illusion* of external guidance. I can certainly see the appeal of that."

Thus, being a Spiritual Eclectic is sometimes just too much damned *work*. Edward writes, "Being responsible for beliefs you formulate for yourself from many world traditions is daunting for many, who find it much easier to simply accept a set of dogmatic beliefs handed to them by a traditional church."

Marmot laments "questions and accusations to deal with from authority figures, requests for donations from places you wouldn't believe—and whose adherents couldn't stand to be in the same room together. There is not enough time to practice everything I could preach. Spiritual life can be complex and over-stimulating, just when I need something simple and soothing."

Conclusion of Case

Mike was very aware of Maya's anxiety, but he felt very calm himself. The dryness she was describing is common to most people on a spiritual path and is in no way the exclusive experience of Spiritual Eclectics. But John of the Cross was not going to be terribly helpful here—Mike (himself a Liberal Believer) knew that he would need to address it in terms most helpful to his client.

He took a piece of paper and a big magic marker out of his desk. He drew a large circle and then, with a deft twist of his wrist, drew a stylized "S" inside the circle, dividing it into a pair of one-eyed tadpoles chasing each other's tails. "Do you recognize this?" He asked.

"Of course, that's the symbol of the Tao."

He colored one of the tadpoles black and then filled in the "eye" of the white tadpole. "Right—yin and yang." He pointed to the white tadpole. "Tell me about yang."

She blew air through her cheeks, wondering what this had to do with the matter at hand, but she trusted Mike and so went along with it. "Yang is the active force in the universe. It's busy-ness, activity, growth, motion, stuff like that."

"Good. Now tell me about yin." He pointed to the black tadpole.

"Yin is inactivity, rest . . ." She stopped mid-sentence and stared at the drawing for a long moment. "Spirit isn't gone, it's just . . . quiet." Her eyes began to well up. "I think I only really know where to look for Spirit in its actions, in what it *does*. Maybe I'm missing what it *is*. . . ."

"'And on the seventh day, God rested.'" Mike smiled at her, "But what does God look like when at rest?"

She smiled back at him. "I think I know the answer to that."

Spiritual Eclectics see the Divine at play in all things—all peoples, animals, plants, planets, and stars. Their path is to view themselves as part of this great and holy Whole, and they are invested with a sense of responsibility for protecting the integrity of the Web of Life, the fragile biosphere that gives us birth and sustains our life. Those guiding Eclectics must be sympathetic to their egalitarian values, unoffended by their iconoclastic impulses, and open to their wide-ranging approach to spiritual authority and imagery. For Eclectics, spirituality is always an adventure, and guiding them can be quite a journey in itself.

Spiritual Eclectics At-a-Glance

1. *How is the Divine imaged?* As a spiritual force animating all of nature.
2. *What is the nature of one's relationship with the Divine?* Pantheistic—there is no distinction between creation and the Divine.
3. *How does one construct meaning in the world?* By protecting the biosphere and all creatures, and by promoting greater consciousness.
4. *What are the accepted sources of spiritual wisdom?* Spiritual wisdom of every tradition, in one's own experience, and in the body.
5. *How is spiritual growth assessed?* The degree to which one can see through the illusion of separateness and realize one's unity with all being.
6. *Practices?* Prayer, meditation, ritual, sacred reading, art, exercise, being in nature, and activism.
7. *Advantages?* Diversity and spiritual generosity.
8. *Disadvantages?* Gullibility and a lack of groundedness.

3
Ethical Humanists

Aaron is proud to be a card-carrying atheist. He is even eager to take his card out and show it around when the opportunity is right. He showed it to Meg, his existential coach, on his very first visit to her. Since Aaron is an atheist, it did not occur to him to go for spiritual guidance, nor would it make sense to him if someone had suggested it. But Meg is a shrewd businesswoman and has printed up different cards to target the different communities she works with. Aaron doesn't know that the techniques and methodology Meg applies in their sessions comes from her training as a spiritual guide, but she has all the skills and tools necessary to be a good existential coach, and this is what Aaron expects of her.

Aaron originally came to her to help him cope with the loss of his wife to cancer. His grief did not dissuade him of his certainty that there is no God—a belief he has held since high school—but indeed reinforced it, as Aaron is sure that no all-loving, all-powerful being would permit such suffering. But working through his loss inevitably led him to an examination of his own existential issues. A railroad enthusiast and a bit of an eccentric, Aaron sometimes wore his conductor's cap to session.

He wore no cap when Meg called him into her office one blustery October day. "No train to drive, Casey Jones?" Meg asked, settling into the chair opposite him.

"Off the rails," he looked at his feet. "What's the point, Meg?" She cocked an eyebrow at him, which he knew meant, "Tell me more."

"The other day I was downtown, train-watching with the guys." Like birdwatchers, train watchers "shoot" their prey with cameras and keep detailed records of sightings. "We followed the tracks south and found a kind of graveyard. A train graveyard, that's what Bill called it. Really, it was just a couple of old cars gathering rust. But it got me thinking. These beautiful cars, once they were shiny, racing along the rails. And now they're rusting away, falling back into the earth, flake by flake." He paused for a few moments, still studying his shoes. "I'm just like those cars. Flaky!" He looked up to see her laugh, but his own smile barely covered the pain he was feeling. "I'm going to melt away, atom by atom, until there is nothing left of me, and nothing to remember me by. It will be as if I had never been."

"How does that make you feel?" Meg asked.

"Well, it's a mixture. I feel sad. I wish I could believe in a God, so I could at least have the comfort of self-delusion. But I know that once this old engine stops, everything I am will just rust away into dust. So . . . sad. I feel sad. On the other hand, I feel oddly liberated and relieved. I don't have to worry about hell, or judgment, or any of that other nonsense. I simply am what I am, and then one day, I won't be. There's a rightness to that. It's appropriate—at least, it feels that way."

"Does it make you angry?"

"No, who should I be mad at? Only myself for waiting thirty years to kick the cigs. And . . . well, I wish I had had kids, so a part of me could go on, you know? Not that I'd make a very good father, as Patty used to remind me from time to time."

Meg kept silent and just sat with him for a few minutes. The silence felt portentous and strangely comforting. Finally, he broke it, "I don't want to die without doing something that *matters*."

Ethical Humanists are those who cannot accept the notion of a God or gods whose will upholds and directs the universe. Many of them consider deities to be in the same category as Santa Claus or the Easter Bunny, figments of our collective imagination that persist because there is too much that is unknown, and also because the existential burden of death is simply too great for most of us to bear. Humanists do not believe that God created humans in his own image, but that humans created the gods in ours. Ethical Humanists may describe themselves as atheists or agnostics (of a decidedly non-religious nature), but that does not mean that they are devoid of a discernible spirituality—though most would probably balk at that term. Many of those who responded to the survey identify themselves as "Brights," a fairly new and increasingly popular movement of humanistic atheists and agnostics.

As their name implies, Ethical Humanists are not lacking in ethics. Although many people of more religious persuasions might argue otherwise, Humanists believe that ethics are possible distinct from divine mandates. As Katherine describes, "I think ethics are more important than morals. We need to base our government and societal rules on ethics because morals are so changeable. I think people do horrible things in the name of morals that they wouldn't do if they thought about how they would feel if someone did those things to them." Kit voiced a similar view: "Many religious people feel that morality comes from God—from religion. I don't believe that that is true, even for them. I believe that everyday wisdom and ethics comes from the people responsible for your upbringing. Religion then comes in and takes the credit."

Though eschewing transcendent sources to ground their ethics, Humanists nonetheless have a keen sense of right and wrong, often based on the most primal of motivations, as we shall see. This style is similar to Fowler's "Individual-Reflective" faith, Peck's "Skeptic-Individual" stage, and Schwing's "Humanistic" orientation.

Divine Image

Asking Ethical Humanists about their image of the Divine is a thankless task, as there is no satisfactory answer to what is, from their perspective, a very unsatisfactory question. Nevertheless, the Humanists I queried were good sports and after some grumbling returned a number of responses. "I would never use a word like 'the Divine' (especially not capitalized)," Leo from the UK told me. "All notions of god(s) or the 'spiritual' are just products of the brain."

Raul from Kentucky gave an answer that was almost pantheistic: "The Divine presents an image already, that of invisibility and silence. This squares with the God of the Deists. If anything, I personally imagine the

Divine as being everything that exists, or might: a mulitiverse of infinite dimensions—this is the body of the Divine." Nathan, from California, is also willing to concede a sort of transpersonal reality, but not one that looks like anything offered by the standard religious traditions: "I don't imagine there is a 'Divine'—if anything, to me, there may be some confluence of the 'spirit' of all humankind that, combined, constitutes into some kind of force-of-nature, but I would not say that it has anything like free will."

Ethical Humanists generally do not point to a divine intelligence behind the universe, but they do identify something as holy: life itself. As Katherine writes, "I . . . revere the earth for providing all that I need for life. As such, I do picture the earth to be a sort of Mother/Female—not a loving being, but a force that connects everything on it." Leo agrees, writing, "I am a big fan of Lovelock's Gaia hypothesis as a means of understanding the world and our place in it," referring to a popular theory that views the earth as a living organism. Leo clarifies, "but not in a 'Mother Nature' sense attributed to it by people who don't understand it and use it to suggest a greater meaning than the interaction of organisms and natural systems."

That life exists in the universe is so incredibly unlikely as to be miraculous—the improbability of human life and consciousness is not lost on Humanists, and they have an orientation of awe toward it. They do not pray to it or consider it conscious in any regular sense of that term, yet they serve it through their efforts to preserve the environment and to protect the rights of both animals and human beings.

As Quincy from Washington, D.C., writes eloquently, "The 'Divine' . . . is the profound mystery of existence, shared by all things. I imagine that this universally shared identity leads to certain human behaviors that reflect divine, rather than selfish, motivations. A good example is my sense of compassion for fellow beings, which sometimes leads me to act in ways that do not serve my personal interests in any way—yet I feel some urge to do so, which seems to defy attempts to justify it solely in evolutionary terms. I believe the theory of evolution is valid and explains most phenomena in the macro world in which we dwell, but I suspect this underlying identity of existence transcends the macro world and manifests itself at times. . . . All humans experience this bond, to varying degrees. Manifestations of it, such as purely compassionate behavior, are instances of how the Divine acts. As for how the Divine 'looks,' you got me. I think visual appearance is a phenomenon of the macro world, which the Divine transcends, so the Divine doesn't have an appearance in any meaningful sense."

Relationship with Divine

Most Ethical Humanists do not recognize the dualism of matter and spirit. As Quincy describes it, "The closest thing to a personal Divinity I can imagine is myself—not to be arrogant and claim to be god, as I am no more or less divine than all other existent things. My own experience does give me at least a slightly greater empirical basis for my own existence than for any other. Yet, my intuition (bolstered by some theories lately advanced by physicists) suggests to me that I am an emergent property of the fundamental 'stuff' of the universe, namely, existence itself. Therefore, my only relationship with the Divine is like that of a ripple to a pond—at once both a property of and also synonymous with the pond itself."

When I asked Leo to describe his relationship with Divinity, he replied, "Non-existent and unnecessary. The most powerful experience is spending time in nature and realizing how insignificant we are in the whole scheme of things." Nathan's answer was similar, but he used an amusing image to describe it: "For better or worse, if there is a force, I'm a leaf in its rain-swollen gutter."

All that we normally think of as "spiritual" is not, for Humanists, a distinct category of existence, but simply the result of electrical and chemical processes inherent in biological systems. Since there is no heaven for them that outweighs the importance of the earth, this world is afforded their ultimate concern. This is the only planet we know of where life exists (certainly in such staggering diversity), and the preservation of such life is of paramount importance. Ethical Humanists do not see themselves as separate from this life, but indeed, as that part of life that is self-reflexive and conscious of its own being. As Katherine wrote, "I feel that I am one with everything on and of the earth and universe. I am no more or less important than anything I live with, and I have a responsibility to care for my world because otherwise I would not be able to live."

Thus, Humanists practice a form of nature mysticism that is not dependent upon any supernatural agent, but see themselves as one with the earth, a result of self-organizing evolutionary processes.

Meaning

The result of this mysticism is great awe, and a humbling of the human person before the vastness of the cosmos. Unlike many religious traditions that posit humanity's centrality to the cosmic scheme, Ethical Humanists reject such hubris and see themselves as just one of many millions of species, each with an equal right to thrive. If anything, human beings, because of our self-reflexive capacity and thus our power to wreak destruction on the biosphere, have a heightened responsibility toward other species on this planet to preserve and protect them. This responsibility is the basis of the ethics central to a Humanist's spirituality. Though some faith traditions would argue that ethics are impossible divorced from religious revelation, Ethical Humanists would counter that life itself dictates our ethical responsibilities and gives our lives shape, direction, and meaning.

Katherine describes the meaning in her life at length: "I try to be the best human I can. The meaning of my life is what I make of it. I could live day to day (and for long stretches, that is exactly what I do) without doing much of anything besides what it takes to get through the day. But I choose to add meaning/purpose by having children and raising them to be loving, responsible humans, being a wife and friend to my husband, a loving daughter and sister and friend. I take my kids outside and show them our pond and the life that is thriving in it and try to teach them the beauty that can be found in everyday things. We encourage music and art and imagination in our daily lives. I take the bad that comes my way without lamenting 'why me?' because I don't see myself as being more or less special than anyone else, and I don't give thanks to a god for what I have because I don't think it was given to me—I just accept and am grateful for the opportunities that have come my way.

"I was a science major, and I think my 'faith' comes from looking at the makeup of the world from a scientific stance. We are made of elements. At our most basic, we are all the same. So I live my life and give it meaning by remembering that. I don't worry about where I came from—I believe in the big bang theory and believe that I am descended from blue-green algae, but I don't know for sure, and firmly believe that we, as humans, will never have proof of our origins—so I don't sweat it. I don't think I am here for a 'reason' and I don't believe I will 'go' anywhere after death. My body will deteriorate into its basic parts and be recycled. So I guess the short answer is that my faith gives my life meaning by teaching me to take what I can and live the best I can while it lasts."

Still others find meaning in the pursuit of knowledge, the advance of science, and the intellectual mentoring of others. As Karl in California describes, "For me meaning is provided by learning all I can, and since learning is inevitably teaching as well, teaching the things that will make my group flourish. As the group flourishes there will be more free time for teaching, learning, and bonding, and more individuals to choose from for these activities. As a result, my life and the lives of those around me become richer, and we have time to 'smell the flowers,' sing the songs, and enjoy the spirituality of a meaningful existence."

Dologan from Mexico City steers clear of great ethical principles and describes meaning in his life in a way that can only be described as Epicurean: "In a view devoid of higher purpose, the only things that make sense to me are the search for pleasure (in any of its various forms) and the avoidance of pain (of whatever sort). Human capacity for forethought, learning, and rational action should be enough to realize that unrestrained indulgence of immediate pleasures and a cowardly evasion of all pain are not strategies likely to result in an overall maximum of pleasure in the long term: sacrifices will be necessary to reach higher. Moreover, recognition of ourselves as interdependent members of the immense group of similar entities that is the human species, and acknowledgment of everyone's right to pursue the same goals, should lead us to collectively conclude that activities that seek to increase the pleasure/happiness of one individual at the expense of another or others, is likely to reduce or destabilize the overall 'happiness pool,' resulting in an unsustainable state likely to eventually impact negatively on all members of the society. On the other hand, actions that promote well-being, especially if many benefit from them, will result in an overall positive effect. Rationally bound by these restrictions, my meaning in life comes from the enjoyment of it as much as possible in a thoughtful, maximizing way; while avoiding harm to others and taking pleasure from trying to do the opposite."

However, Humanists are, as their name implies, human, and still struggle with existential issues, as Aaron in our case study clearly does. Because Ethical Humanists do not accept the possibility of a spiritual afterlife, they are as susceptible as anyone else to anxiety in the face of the extinction of their own consciousness. Humanists are comforted by the ultimate naturalness of death, that the matter which makes up their bodies has, in the past, constituted the bodies of countless plants and animals for as long as there has been life here, and will after death live again through innumerable creatures.

Yet the knowledge that one's awareness will cease is hard for most of us. Ethical Humanists like Aaron may need help surrendering to death's inevitability, resigning themselves to the fate common to all life, so that life itself may be nourished and continue into the future in other forms. Aaron does not doubt that he will one day die, but he does grieve that he has contributed nothing of enduring value to the human endeavor, since he has not had children, nor has he produced great art, or advanced the cause of science. He doubts he will be remembered as a great train watcher, and he struggles to identify an activity worthy of remembrance after he is gone.

There is always the possibility, for Humanists, that life has no meaning other than the meaning we humans give it. But that does not mean they are morose—as Kit in England wrote, "I don't expect to find 'meaning' in the world on any grand scale, so it would be a waste of time to look for it. I am content. I don't really look for anything more than that."

Sources of Spiritual Wisdom

For Ethical Humanists, spiritual wisdom is derived from "the Book of Nature" (as Thomas Aquinas called it). Instead of "revealed" truth, Humanists rely upon empirically verifiable evidence rendered by the scientific method, and by their casual observations of their own bodies and of nature.

Naturally, the first thing that the Ethical Humanists who answered my survey did was to object to the category of "spiritual" wisdom. Dologon wrote, "I don't honor any source of spiritual wisdom. However, by understanding 'spiritual' more as 'philosophical/ethical,' I honor any source that bases his/her wisdom on rational arguments and on the understanding of human nature and consequences of actions at many levels."

Kit's answer is more comprehensive, but representative of the view of many Humanists: "Obviously the scientific method cannot be applied in a rigid sense in everyday life, but it does provide a set of questions that can be used to challenge any new idea that presents itself. 'Does this make sense?' 'Is the idea well constructed and internally consistent?' 'Does this fit with the evidence that I am aware of?' 'Does this fit with my existing understanding of the way the world works?' There is one last question that I got from the Richard Feynman. He said that there were only two or three things that he had ever known with absolute certainty. This gave him an open mind on many issues, but more importantly he said that it gave him an appreciation of how much hard work he had had to put in to know something with absolute certainty. So when he saw someone asserting an idea with absolute certainty, he would ask himself this question: 'Has the person presenting this idea really done the work necessary to know that it is true?' I honor sources of wisdom wherever I find them. My parents, Richard Feynman, Douglas Adams . . . and many others. But most of all I honor those among them who have given me the tools to distinguish wisdom from foolishness."

Kent is much more concise, but in the same spirit, when he answers, "E. O. Wilson, Carl Sagan, Richard Dawkins, Stephen J. Gould, Charles Darwin, the fossil record, and geological strata."

Ethical Humanists also listen to and weigh the worth of the observations of others—poets, artists, and philosophers whose insights resonate with their own. There is no "otherworld" from which spiritual wisdom may magically come forth; there is only the careful observation of the only world we have to rely on and our collective ruminations upon it.

Spiritual Growth

Again, the Humanists I talked to balked at the notion of any growth that was worth its salt being termed "spiritual." Yet most of them reinterpreted the question in ways that made sense to them. Leo sees such growth in negative terms rather than positive, which, though creative, is probably not so unusual amongst those who identify as atheists, who define themselves by what they *don't* believe. Leo wrote: "Atheism isn't something that most people 'convert' to quickly. It's a journey of questions that lead to more questions, and probably never ends. You can't give someone an atheist bible (if there was such a thing) and simply say 'all the answers are in here.' The less someone believes or claims to know about this world the more they have 'grown.'"

Katherine's definition of "spiritual" progress relies not on external milestones, but upon one's own internal sense of integrity, or, as she puts it, "how honest I feel I can be about my beliefs." She explains further: "When I was a teenager, I would pray desperately to god, hoping to hear or feel something, but on the outside I was aggressively atheist. I would push it in people's face, daring them to comment or hurt me—as was the case when I was a child. I know that I have grown spiritually because I can now articulate my beliefs without worrying how others will react. I can honestly say that I do not believe in a hell and have no fear raising my children as I do on the chance that I may be wrong and damning them. I don't feel threatened by other peoples' faiths they way I did as a child—although I do feel horribly threatened by our current government and society's push towards a 'united' nation of faith."

Spiritual growth for Humanists is likely to be measured by the degree to which people are aware of, and feel responsibility for, life on this planet, both human and animal, and the degree to which we are willing to insure its sustainability. Positing anything more is the spiritual equivalent of masturbation, possessing no ultimate value beyond our mere amusement.

As Elaine expresses it, "The only difference I see between spiritual growth and psychological growth is that, for me, so-called spiritual growth embraces many more principles, such as humanitarianism, animal liberation, and the environment. So I assess it (whatever it is—I'm not really sure) by the extent to which one sees the world beyond oneself and, at the same time, sees oneself as part of the entire world."

Kit also reframes spiritual progress in terms of psychological health. His answer is long, but insightful: "I think that the most important aspect of psychological growth is the growth of empathy. Young children are self-centered and demanding. To them, everything in the world should be directed to their immediate gratification—nothing and no one else matters. Strangely, we can find this endearing. If an adult displayed the same attitudes, we would view them with horror, disgust, or perhaps pity for their mental deficiency. . . .

"As I look at the world now, I believe that it is the failure of empathy that is at the root of all (or almost all) evil. The 'them and us' attitude allows con men to steal from the vulnerable, it allows men to be violent to women, and it allowed the Nazis to commit genocide on the Jews. Everywhere you find evil, I suspect that you will find someone not trying to see the world from another person's point of view. . . .

"It takes a conscious decision to reject the 'them and us' attitude and constant vigilance to put that decision into practice. Watching the news, it is very easy to hate those who perpetrate violence, or to take sides in a conflict. Where someone has shown no empathy for someone else, it requires a real effort of will to think of them as human. And yet I believe that it is important to make that effort."

But this is not a call to sacrifice oneself for the good of the whole, either. Humanism honors all life, including one's own, and the goal is to discern a way of living that is balanced and healthy for oneself as well as for other creatures. This means Humanists do not sacrifice other creatures for their own comfort, but neither do they martyr themselves. Part of discerning a healthy life is making sure that creatures have what they need to thrive, including the human creature: safety, community, nourishment, and love. Humanism supports the pursuit of happiness, insofar as it is ethically sought (i.e., not at the expense of others).

Practices

By and large, the chief practice for Ethical Humanists is philanthropic service and activism. Leo wrote that activism is "something I do value and try and do a lot of. It's also something that makes others appeal to me—and those that have opinions but never do anything about them tend to frustrate the hell out of me. Social/environmental responsibility is something many people ignore and should be taught more in schools. It's easier if you're religious (as I used to be)—live a good life and get the reward in the next one; be nice to people, go to church (etc.), don't rock the boat, give to charity every now and again—and achieve sod all. Really trying to bring about change means challenging the way our world works and being prepared to ask difficult questions about our ideas and lifestyles—even if we don't always make the changes. (I actually find many conflicts between my lifestyle and what I'm trying to achieve—mainly because of the amount of meetings I go to.) Maybe the need to challenge the accepted explains why so many activists I meet are agnostics, atheists, or, in the case of the Pagans I know, sympathetic to non-religious ideas."

Almost as important for Humanists as activism and service is spending time in nature and immersing oneself in the wonder of the mysterious cosmos. Kent also tries to study the natural sciences as a way to deepen this connection. He says he reads to "foster a sense of connectedness with nature. I study science, biology, geology, ecology, cosmology, physics, and even computer science (everything computes). This gives me an intellectual foundation for experiencing awe at nature and the cosmos. To do this I often go out hiking by myself. When I am out there in nature, by myself, and I think long and hard about nature, all [of the] things I learn in books seem to meld together and they inspire great emotion in me." He enjoys "a sense of intense awe of nature, the cosmos," and the remoteness of "the probability that I am even here, and even more so, conscious." For Elaine, this connectedness to nature is expressed through gardening.

Humanists are also great fans of art and literature and find reading and study a satisfying practice. Leo does not limit this to scientific sources, but loves science fiction, as it "allows people to play with ideas that may become real issues or be comments on real issues—think what Arthur C. Clarke has predicted, and Kim Stanley Robinson's Mars trilogy is a comment on different types of revolution and social change (armed struggle through to velvet revolution)."

Finally, ruthless self-examination is important to Humanists. This may partly be a reaction to the "corporate delusion" of religion, but is also a heartfelt commitment to realistic and verifiable truth. As Raul describes it, "I seek internal integration . . . to promote self-trust at all levels of my mind. This brings the conscious and the intuitive much closer together. Aggressive internal truth-telling at the expense of superficial self-comforting, that's the ticket. To pare everything—conditional and human—away and see the universe as-it-is. Truth is the key to spirituality; if it ain't true, what damn good is it? But truth cannot be grasped passively. It will not drift in through your transom. In a sense, the process of truth-seeking is a process of intentional ego destruction."

Advantages

When I asked about the advantages of this style of faith, Leo responded, "It's not a faith or belief (and that's an advantage in itself). Freedom of thought and of speech, constantly evolving and challenging, no indoctrination, rituals, or leaders, and no godhead to answer to."

Far from the stereotype of the cold and angry atheist, Ethical Humanism demands an orientation of awe toward the cosmos that is deeply affective and can motivate those who hold this style of faith toward compassionate action on behalf of themselves, other people, other creatures, and the earth itself. Kit elaborates, "I am happy to believe in a world governed by physical laws. I feel wonder and awe at the complexity of life that has arisen from these simple laws without the intervention of any kind of intelligence. To believe in such an intervening intelligence would somehow devalue the beauty of what has arisen through the processes of evolution alone; it would be in some way 'cheating.' And I am spared the mental contortions that must be necessary to believe in a fair, just, and loving God in a world with war, malaria, and the Indian Ocean tsunami."

Katherine also sees advantages in terms of the natural world: "One of the main advantages to my faith is that I don't see myself as special. I have no divine right to use the earth however I want. I don't get to run over to Israel and push the natives into my way of thinking—by whatever means possible. I don't feel guilty about eating meat because I recognize the carnivore in me and I see the naturalness of my lifestyle. While I don't see myself as being better than the animals and plants, I recognize that they are not better than me, so I don't kill myself trying to protect nature above my kids, and if I have to cut down a tree, I just make sure to plant one somewhere. I can be proud of my accomplishments without believing that some divine being gave me the ability to achieve them. I can take responsibility for what I say and do without fear of hell or the promise of heaven."

Kent wrote, "The advantages to my worldview are that I am no longer psychologically imprisoned by superstition and supernatural paranoia. I no longer blame Satan for bad things I do, or worry about God's view of me. I answer to myself and fellow humans. I see nature clearly and stand in awe of probability and the cosmos. I can know with great certainty that science offers the truest knowledge to be had by our species."

In holding only to that which is scientifically verifiable, Humanists avoid the problems of official dogma and required belief that can plague other styles. Freed from the specter of judgment, one can be at liberty to truly act in the world in ways that make sense to each individual, rather than being coerced into nonsensical behaviors motivated by what they see as a collective delusion. As Elaine put it, "It is based on truth more than illusion; it is broad and inclusive; it is flexible."

Freedom appears to be a theme in the responses. Vic wrote, "I feel I'm free to examine the world with an open mind and not be bound by doctrine and ritual. It gives you a real sense of inner freedom. You are free to explore other ways of thinking and are free to see the universe for yourself without someone or some group telling you what it all means."

Disadvantages

The chief disadvantage described by those who answered the survey was the prejudice others show toward those who hold no religious beliefs. Almost all the respondents touched on this, but Leo perhaps said it best when he objected to "the way others see atheists/humanists/Brights/etc.—all negative language. Why must we be denying or without something they can't prove exists? We live in a very faith-orientated society, yet non-theists are the second largest philosophical group and very little provision is made for us. We're accused of a whole range of things (most recently and unfairly, racism) when we question or joke about the beliefs of others, yet believers have this wonderful 'wall of faith' to hide behind when defending their (often ridiculous) statements. Religion should be as open to question and jest as political affiliation. We get called heretics, non-believers, infidels, etc., condemned to hell, and (the worst of all) we have people saying they'll pray for us—all of which are highly offensive."

A few of the respondents also mentioned the lack of community or some other forum for support. Raul mentioned this lack of community, but then was quick to add, "all humanity is my community and my family. This is a very uplifting point of view, but it must be acknowledged that *as* a family the world is acutely dysfunctional." He continues, lamenting the lack of leadership: "There is no one to whom I can turn for spiritual advice. I do not accept in principle that such advice can ever be valid or meaningful. I am alone in facing the universe and determining my relationship to and place within it. While I am listing this as a disadvantage, it is a universal and necessary one. Needing air to breath is another such disadvantage."

Katherine laments this lack of community as well, but worries more for her children than for herself: "The main disadvantage is that I have very little support. No church to run to that will tell me I am raising my kids properly or how to act. No Divine making decisions for me and taking the responsibility from my shoulders. The condemnation of society is a big negative—having to worry about my kids at school if others find out we don't follow the flock. I was tormented as a child, and I don't want that for my kids. I would like to think that I am raising them to think for themselves and that I am open to letting them choose how they will believe. I want them to be honest and friendly when describing how our family lives so that others are more open to them—I believe that my hostile attitude may have contributed to how I was treated."

Another negative expressed by several of the respondants is stated succinctly by Elaine: "It doesn't provide me much hope or confidence." Dologon elaborates: "[A] lack of faith in an infallible, divine 'safety net' may make it more difficult to retain hope and strength in difficult circumstances of fear and pain for some people. Disbelief in a certain, eventual punishment for harmful actions may make morally immature/dysfunctional people feel encouraged to do harm to others (or themselves) for (unsustainable, short-term) personal benefit." Kent seems to agree and concedes that the Humanist position offers "no readily available psychological cushions for suffering and death."

Ironically, however, Humanists can be just as rigid and dogmatic as those of other styles. The old adage, "Scratch an atheist, find a fundamentalist," has an element of truth to it, as many humanists acknowledge. A truly ethical humanism allows others the same freedom for or from religion that Humanists themselves enjoy. The insistence on the ephemerality of individual awareness at death can be a hard burden for most people, but those committed to this path paradoxically find in this a kind of freedom as well.

Conclusion of Case

Meg sat in silence with Aaron for a time. Finally, she spoke softly, "Aaron, did Patty have children before you were married?"

"No. I was her first and only love." His eyes glazed a bit as he remembered her.

"What great work did she contribute to society?"

He snapped back to the present and scowled. "Are you mocking me?"

"Not at all! You know me better than that. Indulge me."

He shifted uncomfortably. "She used to watercolor—but she wasn't very good." He grinned, remembering. "She once did this large portrait of me. It looked a little like a moose!" He laughed and wiped at his eyes. "What are you getting at?"

"What did Patty do that was great? What did she do that made her worthy of such fond remembrance?" Meg asked.

Aaron's voice cracked when he spoke. "She loved me. God knows why, but she did."

"Was her life a waste?"

"God, no."

Meg struggled with what to say. She felt uncomfortable, like she was being too directive, yet she felt a nudge that she could not ignore, so she surrendered to it, leaned in and whispered to him, "Who will you love now, Aaron? Whose life will you bless?"

Ethical Humanists At-a-Glance

1. *How is the Divine imaged?* As life itself.
2. *What is the nature of one's relationship with the Divine?* Unity with all life.
3. *How does one construct meaning in the world?* By compassionate action on behalf of life.
4. *What are the accepted sources of spiritual wisdom?* The natural world, the scientific method.
5. *How is spiritual growth assessed?* By one's commitment to biological sustainability, the protection of existing life forms, including oneself.
6. *Practices?* Activism, being in nature, reading and study (especially the sciences).
7. *Advantages?* Life of awe and purpose free from delusion.
8. *Disadvantages?* Ephemerality of one's own consciousness, intolerance by other faith styles.

The Secondary Triangle

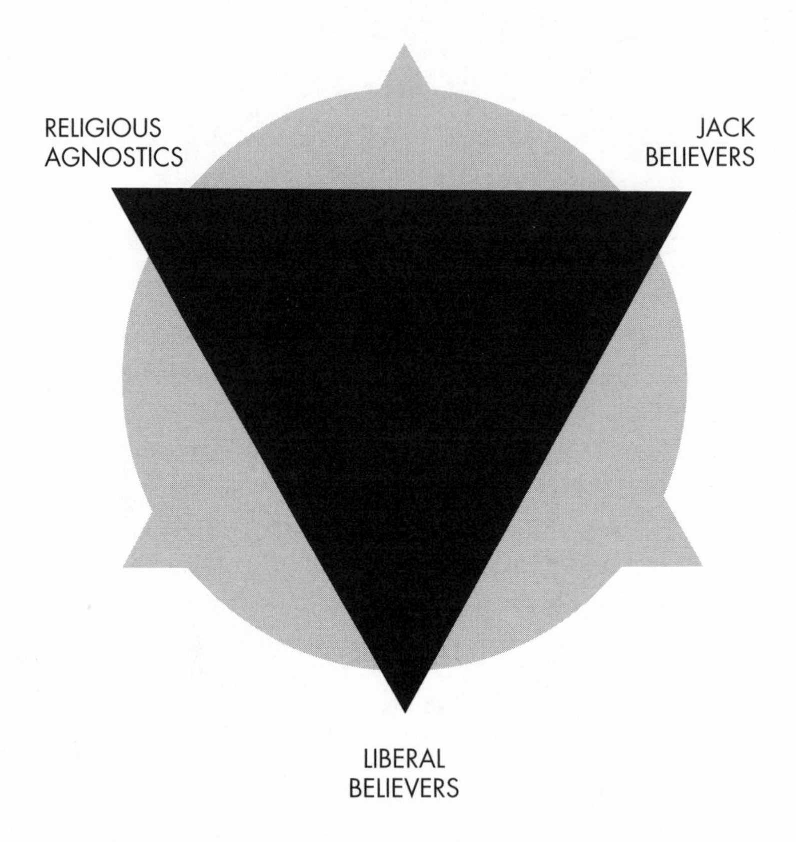

FIGURE 2: THE SECONDARY TRIANGLE

The secondary triangle describes those categories of faith styles that fall in between the points of the primary triangle: Liberal Believers, Religious Agnostics, and Jack Believers. What follows is a description of each of these.

4
Liberal Believers

Ellen sounded tearful and distraught when she phoned Mary Kay, her spiritual guide, rather too late at night for Mary Kay's comfort. She didn't say what was up, but asked for an appointment as soon as possible. Mary Kay said she had an opening the very next morning, if Ellen could be there early.

Ellen was waiting on the steps when Mary Kay arrived. They got settled, lit a candle, and sat for a few moments in silence. Finally Mary Kay asked, "Ellen, what's wrong?" She had noticed that Ellen's hands were red and raw, and she could see her picking and pinching at them as they sat there.

"I got a phone call from my son Jim last night," she said, struggling with her emotions. "He said he wanted to tell me something important when he came home for High Holy Days. I told him I was too busy volunteering at the synagogue for guessing games, and said, 'Just tell me what you want to tell me.' I was impatient—do you know how much work goes into the High Holy Days? I'm going to be running for a week." Ellen had converted to Reformed Judaism when she married Saul, and had embraced it wholeheartedly. When Jim had gone away to college, she threw herself into volunteering for the synagogue, and though she was too modest to say so, May Kay knew through the grapevine that it was Ellen's efforts that largely kept the place going.

"So he just said it, 'Mom, I have a boyfriend.'" Mary Kay could see her reliving the moment; there was a lost and faraway look in her eyes. "I just keep thinking, 'What did I do wrong?'"

"What makes you think you did something wrong?"

"I had to do something wrong, otherwise he wouldn't be . . ."

"Didn't you have some inkling that he might be gay when he was growing up?"

"Well, that's the thing. He says he isn't gay. He says he's 'bisexual,' that he's equally attracted to men and women, that things haven't worked out with girls, so he's going to try dating men instead. Is that normal? That isn't normal, is it?"

Two of Mary Kay's five children were lesbians, so she knew more about the subject than many people. "That's quite a shock, Ellen. But I don't think this is that unusual. Two of my daughters are gay, and one of them dated men for years. Science has shown that most of us are at least potentially bisexual. It seems to me you did a wonderful job raising a son who is comfortable enough with his own sexuality to be true to himself."

Ellen looked at her as if she had suddenly turned into an eggplant. "But what about what God wants?"

"What do you think God wants?"

"The Torah forbids this!" Irritation was then replaced by a true look of horror. "How will I face the other women at temple?"

"This is not about you and your reputation, Ellen. This is about you loving your son right now." It was a slap in the face, but it did bring her around.

"Yes, of course you're right. I just want him to be a good Jewish boy . . . ."

"Ellen, I've been to your synagogue. There are lots of gay and lesbian people there, many of them even have children. They manage to be good and faithful Jews."

"Yes, but none of them are *my* son!" She started to cry.

"Ellen, listen to me. The people of Israel are a very large family. It is big enough to embrace all kinds of people, and it *does*. Jim may only walk away from Israel if you turn away from him. Do you want him to be a good Jew? Why don't you give him the benefit of the doubt and treat him like one, right now?" She paused for a moment and let that sink in. "It seems to me that you are the one struggling with this, not Jim, and not God. Jim and God have their own relationship, and they are both adults, so I suggest we leave them to it. Let's talk about *your* feelings about this. . . ."

Divine Image

Liberal Believers are those who practice traditional forms of faith, but have reinterpreted those traditions in light of scientific progress, textual criticism, and their collective experience of being human. This style is similar to Fowler's "Conjunctive" stage of faith development. Instead of clinging to a divine image born of the Medieval European monarchy, Liberal Believers have democratized Divinity and see it in terms of contemporary political realities. The Divine is less a king and more a friend, companion, and co-worker. Liberal Christians may still pray, "Our Father . . .," but at the same time do not feel like children in the divine presence.

The Divine is less likely to be seen as a great cosmic judge and more likely to be seen as an intimate friend, or even a lover. Scriptural support for this is plentiful: Liberal Hindus can point to the Rasa Dance as an example, Jews to the Song of Solomon, and Christians to the Wedding Feast of the Lamb. In each case, Divinity desires not so much obedience, but intimacy. Tammi, who works at an evangelical mega-church where she sometimes feels theologically out of place, wrote, "I imagine the Divine in so many ways . . . human, Spiritlike wind, loving light, air within and all around, the feeling in my chest and sometimes on my neck. He is so wildly above what I can begin to imagine, but he tells me that he's kind of like a father, like a friend, like a lover, but so much more beyond what I can imagine."

Earl, a Presbyterian in Texas, is almost shocking in his level of comfort with the Divine: "These days, I image the Divine as lover (male) with strong arms, a broad chest, and an energy that grounds and comforts me. My favorite name for God is 'asshole,' but it's meant affectionately and playfully, usually voiced in response to God revealing or deconstructing one of my foibles."

Because their primary response to Divinity is love—with much less emphasis on fear than their Traditional counterparts—Liberal Believers are comfortable experimenting with elements of their faith. Traditional images for God such as Father, King, and Judge can be supplanted by images that are equally grounded in scripture or tradition, but have not had as great a historical following.

Feminine imagery has been especially important as women claim the right of full inclusion in their religious communities. The need to see oneself fully reflected in Divinity is crucial for gender equality, and such alternative divine images as Shekhinah, Sophia, and the Goddess have gained wide popularity in Liberal communities in the past twenty years. As Fran wrote, "The Divine, whom I call God/Sophia, the Universe, Father/Mother, Holy Spirit, Loving Spirit, is imagined in that way and more. I like the saints, and I believe that I can talk to God/Sophia, the Holy Spirit, Jesus, the saints, or the angels without any problems."

Relationship with Divine

Liberal Believers experience more of a level playing field in their relation to Divinity—the Divine is more human and the human more divine in this system. Instead of groveling before a monarch (or kneeling, as some liturgical rubrics instruct), liberals feel entitled to stand in the divine presence. They believe that all human beings (and indeed all creatures) are possessed of an innate dignity that derives not from obedient behavior or from belonging to the "right" group, but from simply being. All things are holy simply because they *are*. As Ken, a pastor in the Reformed tradition, describes it, the Divine is "intimate, personal, familial, yet otherly. I have a sense that God/the Divine is in all places, is all places, is within me, within you, within everything while also being outside and beyond. God is as close to me as my skin, as close to me as the skin of another—so whenever I am with myself, with other, I am with God."

K. D. S., a Buddhist in south-central U.S., agrees: "I am. We all are. Buddhism teaches a basic tenet of 'Buddha Nature' that might best be described as a state of 'Original Virtue' as opposed to 'Original Sin.' Buddhism teaches that the spark of the 'Divine' exists in all beings and that 'wickedness,' or falling short, is learned behavior that arises out of attachment (craving, obsession) with form and the mental creation of dualistic relationships within the physical world."

Liberal Believers are likely to see the evolution of their faith traditions in terms of developmental psychology. They are grateful to have moved out of a literalist perspective they view as an adolescent response to faith into a more adult perspective that reflects what they perceive to be the real ambiguities and uncertainties of life. Tamar, a Jewish woman in Berkeley, California, describes her relationship with Divinity as, "close, loving, desiring, questioning." Such a faith is filled with more shades of gray than black and white directives. Debate and doubt are not seen as threatening to adult faith, but in fact, the very warp and woof of it. When Earl describes his relationship, he writes, "We fight, we wrestle, we flirt—mostly flirt. God communicates with me most powerfully through images and dreams, sometimes in response to scripture. Prayer is ongoing."

The Divine is not a despot to be obeyed in such a system, but a family member with whom one can disagree, argue, and be mad at for a time without any danger to one's soul. Jewish tradition says that God dances when "his" children stand up to "him," and Liberal Believers, by and large, feel much more comfortable doing this than their Traditional brethren. They believe that to be able to do so is the mark of a healthy relationship with Divinity, for if one is not allowed to voice one's disagreement or anger, then one is most likely in relationship with a dysfunctional father figure. But if one is permitted, even encouraged, to confront Divinity with a heartfelt, "What the hell do you think you're doing?" then one has a healthy relationship in which both parties can acknowledge their needs, feelings, and opinions. Beverly describes her relationship with the Divine as being "like a roller-coaster. Long periods of drought, great longing on my part, momentary touches of deep significance. Underlying all that [is] a heart-knowledge of God's constancy. Psalm 139 describes it perfectly." Yet in spite of the conflict and the ups-and-downs, there is a pervading sense of safety and security. As Eddie describes, "My relationship with the Divine is that of love grounded in faith as an acceptance of that which is infinitely loving—even though I can't sense or image what this means, except in metaphor and poetry."

Traditional Believers' relationship with Divinity appears fairly uniform, while Liberals are likely to be highly individualistic in their approaches. While Traditional Believers stress devotional life as the proper pathway to divine union, Liberal Believers honor more diverse approaches. Hindus offer four pathways to Divinity: devotion (*bhakti yoga*), intellectual inquiry (*jñana yoga*), work (*karma yoga*), and psychological/spiritual exercises (*raja yoga*). Liberal Believers of all stripes are likely to recognize each of these and other methods as valid spiritual paths.

Like Traditional Believers, Liberals practice their faith with a whole heart, drawing on the images, language, and iconography of their chosen tradition. Like Eclectics they are likely to believe that what images they use to approach the Divine are more or less arbitrary. Liberals believe that there are many valid paths to the Divine, and *their* way is through their specific tradition. Thus, a Liberal Buddhist might say that his tradition is right for him, but also agree that the Traditional path is proper for others, while Wicca or Judaism or Hinduism is proper for some. Traditional Believers generally believe there is only one way to salvation, while Liberals believe there are many—but *this* way is theirs.

Meaning

Liberal Believers see Divinity and human beings as co-workers in the project of the world. Jewish tradition refers to this as *tikkun olam*, "remaking the world," and views the coming of the messiah as a metaphor for a time when war and inequity have been vanquished and peace and justice truly rule the world. Liberal Christians may understand the second coming of Jesus in very similar terms, and therefore Liberal Jews and Christians share an almost identical eschatological vision for which they can strive together. Liberal Buddhists may understand the coming of Maitreya Buddha in the same way, and again, may work for social justice alongside members of other Liberal faiths.

Fran, a Roman Catholic seminary professor, wrote, "I feel called to understand the pain and suffering in the world in all of its forms, and then know that I have been given the tools to help out, ease some of it by my faith tradition, and by my deep belief that that's what we are all here on this earth to do—to remember our connection to the Divine and all humans and all creatures and all plants, etc., and thus, to heal those parts of ourselves which are parts of it all, as a mother would want to heal her child. To be an educator, activist, and nonprofit system-changer is a great call, but it's one born of faith that this is what I am meant to do to be part of my faith community, and all faith communities."

K. D. S. describes this same sense of purpose in Buddhist terms: "Buddhism teaches that compassion is altruistic and that the mission of compassion is to lift all beings out of suffering. Thus, the ultimate 'meaning' or 'purpose' is nothing less than the liberation of all beings from all forms of suffering—which task is a great joy in and of itself."

In the early twentieth century, which saw the great divergence between Traditional and Liberal theology, this emphasis on justice was named "the

Social Gospel" in the Christian community. It emphasized social sin over personal sin, and activism over personal piety. The phrase "What would Jesus do?" originally comes out of this movement, and was intended to motivate people to institute and support activity on behalf of the poor. Liberals of all spiritual traditions are most often advocates for an increased social welfare system, socialized medicine, equality for gay, lesbian, bisexual, and transgendered persons, and educational opportunities for the underprivileged. Tammi's imagery is moving when she describes her own efforts: "I do what I can to be his love, his hands, feet, mouth, etc., to all those whose lives I touch. I do my little thing. I trust he is ultimately in control and loves me, everyone, and all creation. If I trust . . . I don't have to worry about what is too much for me to understand."

This is also expressed as concern for justice for the planet as well. Beverly writes, "My sense is that we are falling down terribly in regards to our looking after this garden planet. The bottom line is that if we continue to pollute and pillage, life as we know it will end. And what does that say to God? Does that show our love for God? (Let alone any part of God's creation?) Where will our SUVs and shopping malls get us then?"

Ellen, in our case study, was more concerned with how her son's coming out as bisexual would affect her social reputation than how it might negatively impact her son's eternal destiny or his full inclusion in their spiritual community. For Liberal Believers, everyone is entitled to a relationship with the Divine, regardless of sex, ethnicity, social standing, sexual orientation, or religion.

Meaning for Liberal Believers is found in one's participation in this eschatological vision, in "showing mercy, doing justice, and walking humbly" with the Divine, as the prophet Micah put it. Once Ellen works through her personal shame, she may find the courage to confront heterosexism outside herself as well. Advocacy on behalf of her son may prove to be a focus for her efforts toward *tikkun olam*, making the world a more tolerant, diverse, safe, and loving place.

Sources of Spiritual Wisdom

Liberal Believers struggle with the discrepancy between what their traditional and scriptural sources actually say and what reason dictates Divinity must require in a contemporary context. While Traditionalists may view a scriptural text as authoritative for all time, Liberals will want to know the cultural context from which the text emerged, to what concerns it was speaking when written, and will weigh its applicability in light of present circumstances, scientific understanding, and personal experience.

Nevin, a pastor in the Reformed tradition, describes his sources of wisdom as being "Christian, as my core source, but also the wisdom of all other faiths, as well as scientific knowledge as it has been gleaned from the physical and social sciences. I still tend to look at these through a spiritual lens, and one that is grounded in the perspectives of Christianity, especially the mystical/spiritual tradition of Christianity."

This is typical of the responses received, though Beverly is more specific about the "other faiths" she taps for wisdom: "Zen, Sufi, Yoga, Christian Mysticism, *Tao Te Ching*, the Bible, Native American, Thomas Berry's cosmology, nature, poetry, music, family, friends, spiritual directors, my own heart."

It is instructive to note that while some Traditional Believers remained open to the possibility that there may be value in spiritual wisdom from other traditions, not a single respondent actually named a tradition other than their own, and all of them emphasized the need to evaluate this wisdom in light of their primary scriptures. Liberal Believers answered very differently. They were very free with naming specific traditions other than their own from which they derive benefit, and not a single one insisted on the need to square these sources with their own scriptures.

This does not mean, however, that Liberal Believers are not devoted to the texts of their own tradition—indeed they are. They are simply not as likely to view their own scriptures as superior to those of others. As Benjamin from San Jose, California, writes, "I am most deeply immersed in the Bible. I read it as an invitation to participate in archetypal stories of human depth, not as a textbook giving directions. I have deep respect and love for the prayers of Celtic Christianity, the traditions of Judaism, and the nature-honoring dimensions of indigenous earth-centered religions (Native American and Neo-Pagan). I find wisdom in the sacred texts of other traditions (*Qur'an, Tao Te Ching,* Upanishads, etc.) and I am spiritually moved by literature, even when it's not self-consciously 'sacred.'"

Liberal Believers may share the same nomenclature and iconography as their Traditional neighbors, but because of the emphasis on personal experience, they feel at liberty to understand and interpret these in idiosyncratic ways. Betty, a Buddhist from Ohio, lists as her sources of spiritual wisdom the "Eightfold Path, Five Precepts, and the Four Nobel Truths," but she is likely to understand these sources in vastly different ways than her Traditional co-religionists, just as Liberal and Traditional Christians may view the Nicene Creed in ways almost unrecognizable to one another.

Liberal Believers are open to spiritual wisdom not only from their own scriptures and the scriptures of others, they also find value in science and in their own bodies. As Tammi puts it, she balances her sources of wisdom by "a marrying of theology and experience in my practice . . . the idea that my experience is rooted in something I feel to be true, but that my beliefs are more than information and are supported by experience." The Wesleyan Quadrilateral is a fine summary of those sources of wisdom honored by Liberals: Scripture, Tradition, Reason, and Experience, each holding more or less equal authority.

Thus, Ellen in our case study knows that the Torah forbids homosexual activity, but she also knows that science has discovered genetic links to sexual orientation, and she has the lived experience of worshiping every week with gay and lesbian families who are just as active, moral, and dedicated as straight members of her synagogue. These sources cannot help but inform how she ultimately approaches her discernment.

Spiritual Growth

The label "liberal" can mean, in other contexts, *generous*, and Liberal Believers are indeed very generous in their assessment of others and themselves, just as they believe the Divine is generous. Thus, they do not judge themselves or others too harshly and instead choose to believe that the Divine is active in everyone's lives, gently nudging them toward increased awareness, compassion, and wisdom as year succeeds to year. They recognize that the spiritual life will look very different for various people and may even look very different for themselves at various places in their lives. The goal is not to grow into a specific predetermined model (such as one might understand á Kempis' *Imitation of Christ*), but instead to gradually peel away the "false faces" forced upon people by culture, religious tradition, and family expectations so that they may become more and more authentically themselves.

Tammi describes this as a sense of "'belonging' in my own self and as part of the universe." Benjamin adds, "Spiritual growth enables one to move in a wider world, respond more freely to the demands of the world (including being able to refuse to comply with them), respect other traditions not one's own, and to extend concern for justice and fairness to all."

In our case study, Mary Kay sees Jim's coming out to his mother as a huge step in becoming more fully himself, a significant marker in his spiritual growth. This affords Ellen an opportunity to discern and purge the prejudices she may not have even known she held, as well as giving her another avenue for activism.

When, in the survey, I asked how people determined spiritual growth, Beverly answered, "I try not to . . . it is so individual. But if pushed, I would say (paraphrasing Jesus), 'by their fruits you shall know them.'" Tammi understands this in terms informed by St. Paul's "fruits of the Spirit." For her, spiritual growth is gauged by the degree to which she feels "the presence of love, peace, joy, long-suffering, goodness, kindness, meekness in my life."

Many respondents offered some variation on this theme. Nevin explains, in no uncertain terms: "If there is no tangible reflection through acts of love, peace, compassion, devotion, and commitment to the welfare of others and God's creation, then there is no growth. I believe that as a person grows, she or he must manifest her or his spirituality in tangible ways—even if they are very small acts. Like a psychologist, I see improvement as exhibited in changes of behavior and a growing sense of wisdom and awareness of the Divine in everyday life."

Spiritual growth (and even salvation) is thus seen to be a slow, gradual evolutionary process rather than a lightning-bolt experience. Liberal Believers strive for "an adult faith" that recognizes the ambiguities and mystery inherent in the spiritual life and do not need all the answers, all the while trusting that if one can remain faithful and grow into one's true, divinely implanted identity, that some understanding will eventually come.

Practices

Among Liberal Believers, contemplative practice is the order of the day. "Prayer," as such, was almost never at the top of the list, but nestled amongst other activities that foster interiority and quiet. Earl's list contains elements common to most of the respondents: "Insight meditation, *lectio divina*, rosary, studying scripture, corporate worship, Eucharist, labyrinth, time in nature, spoken prayer and silent prayer, chanting, *metta bhavana*, walking meditation, artistic expression, and on and on and on. . . ."

Connection to nature is also very important to Liberals. As Nevin wrote, "I appreciate being in nature, which is a reason we bought a new house on 1.1 wooded acres. It's not just that I like walking in woods and nature, but I like to be surrounded by trees and nature, and when I am, it keeps me more naturally centered." Nor does Deb have to go far to experience this connection: "I garden and for me this is a prayer practice. I have studied the new universe story and want to experience, in a micro way, my little place in the complex web of life. So I take the kitchen garbage, feed it to my worms (composting) who consume it and leave castings. . . . I work the rich castings into the soil to replenish it and plant drought-resistant plants that are both enjoyed for their beauty but also fit into the local ecology of my home spot. This is a prayer practice, as I am cooperating in being the hands of the Divine in bringing forth life. It is part of the rhythm of my week and my life."

Social service also looms large for Liberals. To quote Deb again: "Another part of my life that is like breathing—a non-negotiable—is serving the poor. I commit about ten hours a month to our local homeless agency by being a board member. I volunteer with a wonderful group of people who share my values though not necessarily my religion. The experience of being touched and touching them and together serving our clients is like walking with the living Christ. They (both staff and those we serve) teach me what it is to be a full human person if I have eyes and ears to absorb these lessons of hope, endurance, courage, and laughter."

Although Tammi comes up short in this area, she is conscious of this and acknowledges it: "The 'social justice' things I'm weak on," she admits, but then adds, hopefully, "I give blood and recycle!"

Although there are many commonalities to Liberal spiritual practice, there are many idiosyncratic and distinctive elements in their responses as well. Tamar's list includes "knitting, silence, [and] laughing" while Daniel, an Independent Catholic bishop, adds "working with animals" to his. Both Eddie and Nevin value writing in their daily disciplines. The possibilities for Liberals are endless, as befits a liberal approach to spiritual discipline. Tammi gives the best blanket explanation for this when she writes, "As Jim Finley has said somewhere, it is whatever you bring your whole heart to: playing piano, making love, cooking, embroidery, hiking, simply gazing upon and being part of beautiful scenery, particularly mountain scenery; reading poetry, writing poetry (writing almost anything), sharing deeply with a soul friend, my yoga practice."

Advantages

Liberal Believers benefit from the hope their faith affords them, having found a comfort zone between religious zealotry and scientific reductionism. As Ida told me, "The basic advantage—and reason for—my faith is that I believe it connects me with what is real. Further, my faith gives meaning, hope, definition, and challenge to my life. The advantage of basically liberal belief is that it provides a truer version of reality (I believe), and it provides flexibility." For Daniel, this approach balances both "intellectual understanding and things of the heart." For K. D. S, "It is, at its base, experiential rather than obedience- or knowledge-based. The lessons one has learned 'to the heart' are far more fulfilling than those followed out of fear of punishment or learned 'to the mind' only. It is also very nonjudgmental, looking at actions along shades of being 'skillful' or 'unskillful' rather than a harsh legalistic line between black or white—'evil' or 'good.'"

Liberal faith benefits greatly from its spiritual generosity, allowing Liberals to stand shoulder-to-shoulder with people of other faith traditions working for peace and justice. As Fran describes, "Those people who practice this kind of faith are more open to differences in people, are willing to stretch themselves, don't want to live a life of fear, so they challenge those things that cause fear in themselves and are dedicated to getting out there and helping create good in the world (and peace and justice and more compassion). They call for faith practices (ritual, services, activities, etc.) that support this."

The Liberal hermeneutic of suspicion in regard to scripture and tradition safeguards the relevance of the faith to contemporary culture. And where the two are clearly in opposition, Liberals see opportunity for mutual reflection and correction. In addition, because Liberals tend to value internal authority as having equal weight with external sources, the opportunity for religious abuse is minimized.

Disadvantages

For most of those who answered the survey, the chief disadvantage to a Liberal faith is ambiguity. Betty wrote, "Not everything is clear. As soon as you get an answer to one question, ten more arise due to the answer you just got." Thus, this path is not an easy one to walk. As Fran wrote, "This kind of faith means that you don't have easy black and white answers; it calls for understanding the nuances of life; taking more risks that don't always end well; and living outside the dominant culture of materialism and acquiring things. It takes work."

Ida explains that, for her, "the disadvantage of all faith is that we can't know anything for sure. The disadvantage of Christian faith is its mixed moral history. As for my particular 'kind' of faith, I know—having been fundamentalist in my early years as a Christian—that what I have lost is the elation of certainty, the comfort of having all the answers, and the satisfaction of having a message that is relatively easy to communicate. I don't miss these things."

Ida's concern with how difficult her path is to articulate to others was also widely noted by the respondents. Benjamin wrote, "When the boundaries are not clear, it is sometimes hard to explain (even to yourself) where you stand."

Earl echoed this concern when he wrote that his faith suffers from a "lack of clear answers, doesn't fit well with institutional boundaries and dominant culture, [and is] difficult to express in ways that don't open one to political persecution within the ecclesial organization."

Earl's answer opens another door of difficulty—the fact that Liberal Believers often find themselves at odds with their religious communities, especially when such communities are not as liberal as they. Benjamin explains that, "Openness can often be misunderstood as lack of identity. I find myself these days in very serious conflict with many in my specific tradition (American Baptist) because they are seeking to draw hard lines and defend a certain kind of 'identity' that I find incompatible with genuine spiritual growth. Being intensely personal, my kind of faith is difficult to share in community (though that very challenge is part of why community is important). I can't tell anyone how to make their journey; I can only share what has happened to me and let them make the connections."

Tammi struggles with this as well. She says, "I'm seen as esoteric. Perhaps some people in my church would disapprove of my position if they knew what my faith walk was like. I can be misunderstood. I need to be cautious with what I share with whom—it is just wisdom. I can show them my unique faith by how I live. Because of my fundamentalist upbringing, sometimes I slip back into thinking that I'm 'not doing it right' or 'I'm deceived' or whatever. It takes a bit of discipline to test [God's] heart and mine and know that all is well."

Ironically, though one has trouble fitting in with Traditional Believers in one's community does not mean that Liberals want to be confused with such folk. Nevin writes, "Because I do claim to be a Christian, the assumption by many who do not share my faith is that I'm lumped in with the Jerry Falwells and Pat Robertsons (fundamentalists and literalists) of the world. They think that anyone who is a Christian must think like they do. I am much more a part of the mystical tradition of Christianity, and as a result I am at odds with most of them. Ultimately, the main disadvantage is the inability to speak about my experiences to those who are unwilling to accept my experiences as valid."

From my own observations, I would also like to point out that because of the emphasis on individualistic interpretations and expressions of Liberal faith, Liberal Believers often have a difficult time reaching agreement and making progress toward goals. When everyone's ideas are held as equally valid, if there is a great diversity of ideas, consensus can be an ever-receding goal.

Because of the desire to honor everyone's perspective, understandings that are clearly contrary to the tradition are often tolerated and given equal weight with traditional notions, which can prove confusing to a community's self-concept and also present to outsiders a patchwork-quilt image that may or may not be appealing. In other words, a united front is often hard to establish for Liberal communities, which can impede the effectiveness of their common efforts for social justice and community building.

Conclusion of Case

By the end of their session, Ellen was much calmer and was able to take responsibility for many of her own projections about her son and his sexual orientation. "I guess part of me just doesn't understand how a person could be attracted to *everyone*."

Mary Kay laughed. "I doubt Jim said he's attracted to *everyone*."

Ellen allowed herself a smile, "No, he didn't say that. I just mean men *and* women. I mean, I feel like I have a pretty healthy libido, but I've never had, you know, *those* kinds of thoughts about women."

"Never?" Mary Kay prodded.

Ellen blushed. "Well, I've never let myself *go* there."

"Are you ashamed that Jim has let himself *go there*?"

"I'm not sure if I'm ashamed. I simply expected he wouldn't, out of loyalty, you know, to God . . . to me."

Mary Kay was thoughtful for a moment. "To whom does Jim owe his primary loyalty? To you? Or to the image of God within him?"

Ellen was silent, thinking. Finally, she said, "He has a responsibility to be exactly who he is, even if I don't like it." She glowered at Mary Kay. "And I *don't*."

"That's fine, you don't have to like it. But you do have to *love* him."

"Oh, there's nothing he could do that would make me stop loving him."

Mary Kay said, "Do you know the old rabbinical saying, 'God will hold us accountable for every joy we did not experience'?"

Ellen's eyes widened. "I have heard that, but I never thought about it like that."

Mary Kay winked at her. "Think about it, my dear. Now let's talk about how you can support Jim when he's here for the High Holy Days."

Liberal Believers At-a-Glance

1. *How is the Divine imaged?* As friend, lover, co-worker.
2. *What is the nature of one's relationship with the Divine?* Familial and idiosyncratic.
3. *How does one construct meaning in the world?* "Showing mercy, doing justice, walking humbly."
4. *What are the accepted sources of spiritual wisdom?* Scripture, tradition, reason, and experience.
5. *How is spiritual growth assessed?* The degree to which one is able to be authentically oneself.

6. *Practices?* Myriad contemplative practices, being in nature, social activism.
7. *Advantages?* Spiritual and personal generosity.
8. *Disadvantages?* Difficult to articulate path; lack of focus and consensus.

5

Religious Agnostics

Ted stepped into Gary's office looking like he was ready to cut and run at the first sign of trouble. He was a seminarian at the nearby Unitarian Universalist school for ministry, and though spiritual direction was not required, he thought it might help him navigate some of the inner conflict his studies were arousing in him. Gary was inspired by Ted's dedication to his internal process, his willingness to confront tough questions, and the discipline he was obviously bringing to his seminary experience. Nevertheless, once they got settled and got past the preliminaries, he had a hard time getting started.

"I'm just not sure what I'm doing here."

"You mean in spiritual direction?"

"No, I mean going to school—this school. I'm not sure why I even go to church; why I think I might want to be a minister. I mean, who do I think I'm fooling? I'm not even sure there is a God."

"So what brought you here?"

"I'm just following my nose, I suppose." He grinned. "That rhymes."

Gary grinned back. "But why did your nose lead you *here*?"

"That's just it, I have no idea. I've just been *listening*, you know. This is all crazy. It's just internal nudgings and coincidence. I guess if there is a God, that is how he would work—she, oh, forget it. You know what I mean." He played with the frayed end of his sleeve for a minute. "I think I joined the UUs because it was the only place where I could go to church and not actually have to say I *believe* any of it! I prefer going to Episcopal churches, though. I love the ritual. I just can't say the creeds. I guess there just isn't any place where I feel like I actually fit in. UUs don't have enough ritual or mystery, and Christian denominations expect their ministers to believe and teach certain things that I simply can't affirm."

"So what's the attraction to being a minister?"

"Well, that's complicated, too! Right now I really appreciate the theological study. I may not know exactly what it is I believe, but I get a real kick out of exploring the theological territory. And I really love teaching it, too. I think I like informing people of their theological options much more than I like telling them what they should believe. I guess I'm not alone in this confusion. There are lots of people who are asking the same questions I am. And I think a lot of churches just turn them off, which is a shame, because they have the same needs for community as everyone else."

"Are you talking about other people right now, or are you talking about yourself?" Gary asked gently.

"You caught me." He said, looking up at the ceiling and sighing with mild exasperation. "I guess I'm still trying to find what I need, but I also know there are other people out there who need it, too." He paused. "The UUs come closest to being able to provide that, but in their own way they are just as theologically rigid as other churches."

"How so?"

"You just try talking about your personal relationship with God in my school sometime. Sheesh! Instant pariah." He looked incredibly sad. "I despair that I will ever find a place where I truly fit in."

Religious agnostics are a peculiar group, because alone among all faith styles, their spirituality is ruled not by what they believe, but by what they do not know. This results in a fierce honesty with themselves and others when it comes to matters of faith. Although they are fascinated with the scope of religious traditions, they cannot with clear conscience swallow any of them whole. Like Ted, they may be faithful church members, even clergy, yet there is a nagging ambivalence within that will not let them go all the way to atheism on one side or theism on the other. It is just this ambivalence, however, that is their saving grace, as it results in a rigorous intellectual honesty in both their interior and exterior worlds that is their own brand of faithfulness. "I don't know if there is a God," one might hear a Religious Agnostic say, "but I choose to live as if there is." This is indeed a variety of faith, and in some ways a heroic variety, since it is not one that delivers any certainty or, necessarily, even much comfort to its adherents.

Divine Image

Like their Eclectic neighbors on the wheel, Religious Agnostics are comfortable using numerous images of the Divine, often taken from wildly disparate traditions. They hold them lightly, however, and think of them primarily as metaphors that mediate relationship with something that is essentially unknowable. Earnest from the eastern United States sees three ways of imaging Divinity: "The first is in the sense of god(s)/goddesse(s). These are not at all real beings or real entities—except in that they really do influence and impact people's life. Case in point, I don't see Greek/Roman mythology as anything else other than myth, but I do see truth in it. The ancient world may (or may not have) really believed in their gods/goddesses as existent beings, but obviously modernism (for the most part) killed this way of seeing them. This does not mean that this meaning is actually defunct. . . . The second usage is that of 'God' capitalized, meaning and referring to one specific 'being.' This is what a lot of religious people have in mind when they think about the word 'God,' and it is also what atheists generally think is ridiculous. The problem is that we have painted 'God' into a human definition. This is, of course, an inescapable problem. The only way we could ever possibly talk about 'God' or the 'Divine' is in our own terms. The difference I see between progressives and fundamentalists is that progressives realize this problem and deal with it while fundamentalists insist that their way of talking about 'God' is the right way. For me, this is where I can identify with agnosticism. It just simply isn't my place to insist on all sorts of attributes about 'God' and so forth. But now the third is what I see as an admittance of this. The Hebrews referred to YHWH, the One who is. Or as Marcus Borg puts it, God simply 'is.' In other words, the sum of the parts of existence are in God, yet God is more than existence (*not* pantheism). Or as Paul in the New Testament puts it, it is in God that we live and move and have our being (Acts 17:28). But all of this is not to say that we can really understand how it all works together and fits together. . . . The only knowledge of God one can have is subjective, what they experience of God."

The paradox of relationship with the unknowable is not lost on them. As Bill, from New York, describes it, "Over time, I have come to believe anything that we can define is not God. We can't measure it, count it, contain it, or even name it (not even with a 'secret name'). That doesn't mean we can't talk about it, just that we have to realize we are speculating in symbols or code, and must avoid mistaking 'the pointing finger for the moon.' We hope the word evokes in others what we mean by it."

The metaphor that works best for many of them is "Mystery." Living into Mystery, learning to trust Mystery, and the fostering of relationship with Mystery are achievable goals for Religious Agnostics, though the journey is likely to be full of fitful stops and starts.

Relationship with Divine

This relationship differs from other varieties, too, in that it is difficult for Religious Agnostics to muster much of a sense of devotion. Though great feeling may be present, it is not a feeling of love directed *toward* the Divine so much as it is the feeling one might have for a long-lost love whom one is not sure is still alive, a bittersweet ache nursed within. Ted, in our case study, responds to the ritual of the Episcopal Eucharist specifically because it appeals to this sense of internal longing, yet can't exactly muster the devotion to fully embrace the tradition.

Instead, extroverted practice will more likely take the form of intellectual pursuit and philanthropic service. Natalie, from Mississipi, told me, "I try in all my activities to be a kind and caring person. I want everyone to understand that they are worthwhile and loved people. The only 'Divine' is inside me, and my relationship with it is in the good I do for others."

Likewise, Lutheran pastor Steve, a self-identified Christian Agnostic, wrote, "When I experience compassion, either self-generated or as an observer, I recognize I am in the presence of a divine force." The ecstasy of service or discovery may be poor analogues for the rapture of devotion, but it is what Religious Agnostics have to work with. And if Mystery is conscious and does care about what happens on earth, Religious Agnostics reason, then it will take any service rendered 'unto the least of these' as service unto it. When I asked Ned from the Philippines what his relationship with the Divine was like, he said, "In the sense of being driven to try to improve the world and enlighten the ignorant, pretty intense. In the sense of worship or prayer, nonexistent."

Religious Agnostics may be found in most traditions, often teaching in their seminaries or organizing their soup kitchens. They do not know if Divinity is there, but there is no doubt about the reality of the needs of the poor or the thrill of intellectual discovery.

Many of Ted's professors would probably know well the struggles he is experiencing, if only there were some forum for them to share. Ironically, such existential honesty can be dangerous in seminaries of most faith traditions. Ted is lucky in that the Unitarian Universalist denomination is uniquely oriented toward Religious Agnostics, though he may have difficulty finding opportunity for such intimate exchanges with his instructors.

Meaning

Religious Agnostics are uncomfortable with the meaning handed on by religious traditions, and although they will entertain them, once again they will hold them lightly. If one is not sure there is a God, how can one possibly know God's will? They are also extremely cynical when it comes to the agendas of any faith traditions, as history is chock full of self-interested and even demonic abuses by any tradition one cares to name. As Bill rants, "How horrid, how far from God that people would torture and kill over whether God was one or three? Or whether Jesus was God or *logos* or man or all of these? What do our categories, numbers, or genders mean to God? Lacking nothing, what does God want from us, or is it *for* us? Agreement on creeds? Or love of God and his Creation, especially one another?"

Religious Agnostics consider the notion that one can know the divine will at all to be a dangerous form of hubris, the source of much human suffering, and a threat to the biosphere itself. Thus, they do not take easily to forms of meaning passed on from any tradition.

Instead, they embody a decidedly postmodern perspective that insists that if any meaning is to be found, it must be constructed by each individual from scratch. Thus, for Religious Agnostics, meaning is likely to be less cosmic in scale than for other styles. It will be closer to the earth and easier to verify by hands-on means. As Earnest wrote, "There is no univocal meaning in the world. The only meaning our lives and our world can have is the meaning that we give to it. I have chosen to make an existential commitment to following Jesus. This is what gives me meaning and purpose. Although I cannot say that people in other traditions are without meaning, I can say that my personal observations have led me to the conclusion that meaningful lives come following Christ (that is, living the way Jesus taught us to live; if people in other traditions live the same way then it seems as though they are saying the same things, just in a different spiritual language)."

Natalie finds her meaning in largely existential terms: "My life has meaning simply because it is my life. The good that I do in the world is the manifestation of my belief. My professional career was spent caring for people's physical and emotional needs; my personal life is centered on making my small part of the world a better place to live for all that come through it."

Meaning for Agnostics will also evolve and change as the person him- or herself evolves and changes. What provides meaning for a Religious Agnostic this year may change next year and may take the form of what appear to be baby-step goals to someone of another faith style. As Bill describes his own journey, "I was long trapped in a sort of rationalistic nihilism. Somehow, after some very gloomy teen years, I became and remain convinced that life, with its ups and downs, is getting better, although I didn't connect it to God or faith at the time. Our lives are brief bubbles on an endless sea, tiny flashes of light in the infinite. We matter because we are one-in-a-million accidents of grace who all partake of the Divine. We can either recognize our gift and our connection to the Whole, reflect and magnify the Love we receive, or we can fade out in indifference."

Spiritual guides can assist Religious Agnostics in identifying spiritual goals, brainstorming with their clients how best to evaluate progress toward them, and holding open the possibility that these may need to be reevaluated regularly as the client's relationship with Mystery evolves.

Sources of Spiritual Wisdom

Like Spiritual Eclectics, Religious Agnostics are likely to honor scriptures and traditions from many sources as useful to them, but again, they will hold these lightly. They are all intellectual fodder that may or may not shed light on their existential situations. They may even have favorites among traditional sources, but all sources are secondary to the Religious Agnostic's personal experience. Cathy's response is typical of Religious Agnostics. When asked what sources of spiritual wisdom she honors, she wrote, "Anything, everything, and everyone. You can learn an amazing amount about life by seeing it through the eyes of children, other people, and even animals. When I was younger, I attributed a lot of weight to things like Tarot and old Eastern prophecies, something that could give me an answer when I didn't have enough knowledge or belief in myself to work out an answer on my own. Now that I have lived a bit more, I prefer to just open my eyes and take knowledge from any source."

In giving experience such weight, they will follow Kierkegaard all the way to the cliff, but are not able to make the leap of faith he insists upon. Instead of his "Knights of Faith," we may see Religious Agnostics as "Knights of Doubt." They can see the usefulness of traditional sources, they may even see how they are salvific (in a this-worldly sense) for people of other faith styles, yet to make that leap themselves feels disingenuous. Belief is simply not something they can fake.

Spiritual Growth

Spiritual progress is measured by Religious Agnostics in myriad ways, foremost being their level of existential anxiety. The more anxious one is, the more work needs to be done; less anxiety, conversely, is seen as progress. But this is also paradoxical, since it is this very anxiety that in large part drives the Religious Agnostics' spiritual journey. Some may see the ability to transition into a more theistic faith style as a goal, but most will see spiritual growth in terms of an increased capacity to be at peace in the midst of great internal conflict.

Many see this growth in terms of a shift from egocentric to philanthropic concern—in other words, the ability to consider the needs of others as superior to one's own needs. While one might see this as a universal spiritual goal applicable to most faith styles, the here-and-now nature of such concern makes it primary for Religious Agnostics. Ned said he measures spiritual progress "mainly by social responsibility (especially reproductive responsibility). Also by environmental awareness and concern. Then, knowledge of rational thought and traditions." Natalie agrees, measuring spiritual growth "by the way the people I meet and with whom I interact react to me. Growth is continuing to help my fellow man and trying to make an improvement in the world."

Traditional and Liberal Believers may agree that one should sacrifice for others, but for them the motivator is the will of Divinity for them to do so, while for Religious Agnostics the reward is more immediate and will probably be understood more in terms of psychological development, and only secondarily as spiritual progress.

Cathy sees these two main goals as being related: "I measure my own spiritual growth against my relationships with other people. The older I get, the more I understand other people, the more I empathize, and feel closer. The more comfortable I feel with myself, the more comfortable I feel with other people, the more valuable my relationships become and the more I feel I have grown." Bill offered the most succinct summary of both of these goals: "By an increase in joy and love toward others."

Practices

By far the most frequent answer to this question for Religious Agnostics was time spent in communion with nature. As Cathy wrote, "Nothing makes my soul feel more at peace than being in places of outstanding natural beauty. The rolling hills of Scotland as the sun creeps over them, looking over a lake in the crisp clear morning light. . . . I feel like my spirit is far more related to the physical earth and matter, though I do spend time studying such things as chakras and movement of energy." Earnest relates observing the natural world to Mystery, when he wrote, "Reflecting on the complexities of nature is a great way to point to the existence of that which is greater than all existence that we know."

Natalie affirms the value of nature, but not as highly as activism: "I do enjoy nature because of its beauty, but I do not consider it a manifestation of any supernatural being (biology and botany are not religions). . . . I have always been active in causes to try to improve society (civil rights, antiwar rallies, women's rights), but I have never considered these to be spiritual practices, just expressions of my personal beliefs."

Though some respondents did mention prayer and meditation, it was often in the context of struggle. Such disciplines do not come easy to Agnostics, though much effort may be expended on them. Rose Marie, from Berkeley, California, lists as her chief practice art as a form of meditation: "I find great spiritual satisfaction in doing, creating, and making. I am basically a wordsmith, but I am calmed and made happier in my world by producing things that creep towards my own idea of what is beautiful—whether it's in a watercolor, the design for a multicolored sweater, the arrangement of pictures on a wall, a bookbinding. I never achieve it—but the hours spent working are a spiritual experience rather than labor. I find delight—i.e., a kind of transcendence—when things work out better than I expected. But like the carpet weaver, I know that perfection does not belong to me."

Advantages

This path is a particularly difficult one; nonetheless, many of the respondents were very upbeat about its positive role in their lives. Earnest wrote that his faith is "inclusive, nonjudgmental, and I seek to change myself and to only change others by what they see in me (not convert or proselytize), and I know that, when exercised, my faith gives me meaning, satisfaction, and fulfillment. By remaining virtually agnostic with the entire 'supernatural' question, I can try to relate to people who fall to one side or the other. In other words, I see myself as able to be a bridge between two extreme and opposing views."

Those who walk it do so largely because they can do nothing else and still look at themselves full in the face in the mirror. Bill's faith, then, is valuable because it "offends neither my intelligence nor my conscience." The reward of Religious Agnosticism is the ability to maintain one's personal integrity, while at the same time acknowledging the internal longing for transcendence, however that may be perceived. For Agnostics, it is important to embrace reality in so far as it can be known without giving in to religious dogmatism. As Natalie wrote, "I am able to express myself and my beliefs without having someone such as a priest or minister tell me what views I should have. The ability to face the world without the dogmatic schemes of an outdated, fantasy-based religion." For Dave, the reward is "the ability to see the world as it is. It doesn't dull the joy of discovery to credit nature instead of a god for all that exists."

Cathy sees this great advantage in terms of intellectual generosity. She wrote that the greatest advantage to her faith was "open-mindedness. I have my own ideas, but I'm open to being proved wrong. This means that I will listen to everyone's thoughts—I don't always give them equal merit—but I don't dismiss anyone. This results in a lack of prejudice that follows through my whole life. I suppose I could be accused of sitting on the fence, because I don't side with or against anyone, but it means that I treat everyone fairly."

In this delicate tightrope walk between faith and doubt, neither side really wins out. Such a path requires great intellectual rigor and a painful degree of honesty and may be difficult to sustain for most people for any great length of time. Nonetheless, for some it is an extremely rewarding path, and it affords them an eagle-eyed perspective that allows them to work cooperatively with nearly every other faith style.

Disadvantages

The cost of living with such a high degree of existential anxiety is hard to overemphasize. The balance of faith and doubt necessary for Religious Agnostics to maintain their path is exhausting and may lead one to simply give up and come down on one side of the fence or the other: one person may embrace theism (shot-through with self-loathing as the person knows he or she is lying to him or herself) or atheism (and enter fully into a dangerous existential despair that may lead to self-mutilation or destruction).

Other disadvantages mentioned by the survey respondents include the difficulty in articulating one's faith to others, and the misunderstanding that can result. As Bill put it, "It is hard to define or explain to someone who doesn't already know it (or know that they know it). Sort of like God."

Earnest lamented that his faith "is often prone to misunderstandings, and this can lead to rejection by both 'liberals' and 'conservatives.' There are some who have the impression that I'm an outdated Christian living in the premodern world and that I'm a fundamentalist and that I've got a few loose screws in the head. Then there are others who feel that I'm a flaming oozing cesspool of heresy and unorthodoxy. When I lived in the Midwest, I always felt treated like a liberal and now that I live in New England I feel treated like a conservative. It's hard to always get caught in the middle of culture wars and witch hunts."

For Steve, who works as a Christian pastor, the path of the Religious Agnostic is often "anti-institutional [and has a] tendency to be too individualistic." For Ned, the social responsibility sometimes feels simply overwhelming since, with no certainty of divine assistance, his faith leaves him "feeling responsible for improving life and society, instead of being content with things as they are."

Spiritual guides operating from other faith styles may protest that I am not giving enough impetus to the Divine in this work with Religious Agnostics. While this may be an appropriate consideration for most other faith styles, one must be cautious in thinking this way with this particular style. Mystery may be at work or may not be at work, and any insistence on the activity of divine providence will tip the guide's hand and may make it unsafe for Religious Agnostics to continue the work. As with any client, Religious Agnostics must feel that their guide is on their side and playing by their rules.

Conclusion of Case

Ted spent a long time describing his feelings about being a religious misfit. Gary felt that providing some solidarity with him was appropriate, and so allowed himself some self-disclosure about his own existential struggles. Ted was emboldened by this information, felt less alone in his journey, and was given hope that he might have something of value to offer as a minister. "In my experience," Gary told him, "people are fed up with the party line spouted by their clergy. There are many who find it genuinely refreshing to hear a minister stand up in the pulpit and say he doesn't have all the answers."

"I think that's what I like best about the preaching at UU churches," Ted agreed. "I'm so turned off by the arrogance I feel coming from the televangelists and the preachers I grew up hearing."

Gary leaned in as if whispering to him The Great Secret. "Your honesty and vulnerability are the best tools for ministry that you have."

Ted smiled a half-smile, "Not everyone thinks so."

"Not everyone will appreciate what you have to offer, no. But don't you think there are lots of people like you for whom the televangelists' message is not appropriate?"

"Oh, yeah," he nodded.

"And don't you think that most of them feel just as alienated from religious community as you do? Just as much of a misfit?"

"They must," he agreed.

"That's your flock, then, Ted, and they need you. And there are *millions* of them."

Religious Agnostics At-a-Glance

1. *How is the Divine imaged?* Primarily as unknowable Mystery.
2. *What is the nature of one's relationship with the Divine?* Intellectual pursuit and philanthropic service.
3. *How does one construct meaning in the world?* From scratch, and idiosyncratically.
4. *What are the accepted sources of spiritual wisdom?* Largely personal experience and reason.
5. *How is spiritual growth assessed?* Level of existential anxiety and philanthropic commitment.
6. *Practices?* Being in nature, activism, prayer and meditation.
7. *Advantages?* Personal integrity.
8. *Disadvantages?* High level of anxiety is exhausting.

6
Jack Believers

Russell was a Lutheran pastor in Salt Lake City who was on his way to the annual conference of Spiritual Directors International, held that year in Donaldson, Indiana. He was annoyed to discover, after rushing to the airport, that his plane would be delayed for three hours. He decided to make the best of it with as good a cabernet as he could get in such a place, checked his bag, and walked in to the best-looking bar he could find. It was crowded, as the snow had caused problems for numerous flights. He felt lucky to find an empty table near the back and settled in, trying to catch the waiter's eye. He eventually did, and opened a paperback.

"You don't look happy," a feminine voice offered. He looked up to see a thirty-something woman in a print dress and gray wool coat fumbling with a pack of cigarettes she wasn't allowed to smoke.

"Thank you for noticing. Looks like I'm going to be here for a while, and no, I'm not happy about it."

"Just like life, huh?" She grinned at him. It wasn't a mirthful grin, but a sad and tired one.

Russell struggled with whether to take the bait. The woman obviously wanted—or needed—to talk. He gauged his inner resources: well rested, plenty of time . . . and there was that pesky thing about entertaining angels unawares. "Why, whatever do you mean?" He grinned at his own literary turn and snapped up the hook.

"Buy me a drink?"

"I'm only in it for the drink and the talk."

"Deal." Over the next hour, Marsha and he made small talk, then graduated to revelations about their families, and then work. Marsha was a waitress in Denver, had just flown here to visit her children who lived with their father, and was returning home. She was a little startled to discover Russell was a clergy person. He could tell it made her uncomfortable. "I don't do the God stuff," she said, shifting on her stool.

Russell tried to put her at ease. "No collar, see? I'm off work. Just a normal Joe that loves a good cab."

"That's a little funny, too," she smiled wryly. "Most men who drink around here drink beer."

Russell stuck out his tongue and made a face. She laughed.

"So why don't you do the God stuff?" He asked.

"I don't because I can't." She looked down and played with her coaster. "I'm one of the damned, you know."

"I'm not sure that I do. What do you mean by that?"

"I grew up Mormon, same as everyone else around here—well, mostly, I guess. I tried to do everything right. Tried to find me a good man, got married in the Temple, had me some kids. I did it all *right*, you know?"

Russell nodded. He had lived and worked amongst the Mormon majority here in Utah for most of his adult life. He knew the drill. "What happened?"

"My husband cheated on me. I caught him, bastard. Caught him in our own bed. I threw a vase at them both and hit her square between the eyes. Knocked the bitch out cold. Needed eighteen stitches. He painted me as crazy, lied to the police, and divorced me. Took my babies from me, too. Bastard." She played with her cigarettes some more. "So now I got me a criminal record, no kids, and a taste for the fire water. Lucky me."

Russell looked at her with compassion and waited for her to continue. "So I've lost my place in the Celestial Kingdom. Hell, I'm not even one of you poor souls, you people who think you're religious but are only going to the Terrestrial Kingdom. I'm headed straight for the Telestial, the lowest of the low."

Russell was familiar with Mormon theology, which viewed the afterlife as a three-tiered arrangement of worlds. The Celestial Kingdom was the

Mormon heaven, where one goes until one is granted his own universe to rule (or to help with, if a woman). The Terrestrial Kingdom was where all those righteous people of other religions wound up, so that they can have another opportunity to hear the Mormon gospel. The Telestial Kingdom was for everybody else. It wasn't as bad as the Catholic or Protestant Hell, but it wasn't a cheery prospect, either.

"So did you stop believing in God?"

"Nah, I believe in God. I just don't think God believes in me." She looked like she might cry. "I don't measure up, you know? Mormons got a lot of rules, maybe you guys do too, I don't know. Too many rules for someone like me to follow, after all I been through. I'm damaged goods, you know what I mean? There's no place for me with God. He might love me, but he *sure* don't like me."

Marsha is a Jack Mormon, the name given to those who believe in the Mormon faith, but for some reason cannot exist within it. Perhaps, like Marsha, they have missed their chance for the ideal Mormon lifestyle, or perhaps they are addicted to one substance or another, are gay or lesbian, or are those who have been rejected by their families for not conforming in some other way.

Other varieties of religion have their "Jack" followers, too (known in some communities as "backsliders" or "apostates"). Like Traditional Believers, they assent to the tenets of a tradition's orthodoxy, but unlike their Traditional neighbors on the wheel, cannot, for one reason or another, live by the rules such orthodoxy demands. They do not feel at liberty to migrate to any other points on the wheel, since the orthodox dogma they share with their Traditional neighbors does not recognize the validity of any other faith style.

This is undeniably the saddest point on the wheel. While all of the other points have things to recommend them, and can all be healthy responses to the Divine, the Jack Believers alone are utterly unenviable. Their relationship with the Divine has been severed both by the exterior condemnation of their religious traditions and by their own internalized sense of damnation.

It is not likely that such persons will seek out spiritual guidance; nonetheless, like Russell, most of us will come in contact with them now and again. Although it is not likely we will sway them from their self-condemnation (since to do so would mean invalidating their belief system), we may find opportunity to show them a kinder and more compassionate response to the Divine than they have experienced before, if only by example.

Even after asking literally hundreds of people, not a single Jack Believer answered my request to fill out a survey. This is not at all surprising. Jack Believers are not proud of their orientation—it is far too painful to reflect critically on their faith, since it is mostly a record of loss. Therefore, for this chapter, we will have to rely not on actual words from Jack Believers, but upon the example of people I have known, or known of. Their identities have been masked, and some are composites, but all of the situations—and all of the pain—are real.

Divine Image

The Jack Believer's universe looks very much like that of the Traditional Believer, yet the mercy with which divine justice is tempered is in short supply. Divinity is seen primarily as judge, and the Jack Believer views him- or herself as the condemned. Marsha put it mildly in our case study, when she said, "I believe in God, I just don't think God believes in me." While their Traditional neighbors on the wheel view the Divine as a benevolent father, Jack Believers are the rebellious sons and daughters that carry the collective shadows of the Traditional Believer's community.

Justin is a good example. Although his parents take the "tough love" approach to religion, Justin only does what he absolutely has to do. He believes their evangelical Christian faith is all true, but the association between his punishing stepfather and punishing deity is cemented into his imagination. Famous in his youth group for climbing out his window at night to party with the public school "burnouts," Justin knows he can't "sneak around" on God—since God truly does see everything. But that doesn't stop him from acting out at church in the same way that he does at home. His parents must check with the youth pastor after every service to see if Justin skipped youth church or not. The fact that they regularly tell him what a terrible son he is feeds his feelings of unacceptability both to God and to his stepfather.

His stepfather is an arch-conservative evangelical who also feels unacceptable to God. He considers his stepson to be God's judgment upon him and beats Justin without mercy, feeling he is fulfilling the divine mandate, "Spare the rod, spoil the child." The Traditional Believer and the Jack Believer are the only two points on the wheel that are psychologically dependent upon one another, and unfortunately the relationship is a dysfunctional one, and highly destructive to the Jack Believer's psyche.

Relationship with Divine

The Jack Believer's relationship to the Divine can only be described in negative terms. They may experience a continuum of alienation, ranging from estrangement on one end to perceived banishment on the other. "God might love me," Marsha told Russell in our case study, "But he *sure* doesn't like me." These are psychological states on the one hand, but can also be physical realities on the other when the Traditional Believers actively shun the Jacks.

Judith got pregnant when she was fourteen, and when her Orthodox Jewish father found out, he threw her out onto the street and declared her "dead." Her room was emptied of its contents, littering the street with cardboard boxes with "Free" signs scrawled on their sides in magic marker. Judith found her way to a homeless shelter, where she was supported and encouraged to go to a women's services agency. The agency found her prenatal care and a place to live. But the wounding to her psyche was harder to heal. Well-grounded in Jewish thought, Judith believed that because of her father's rejection, she had been cast out from her people as well, and therefore was cut off from the inheritance of Israel. Her connection to her people, her identity, severed, she did not know who she was, or where to look for direction.

Judith was counseled by an interfaith chaplain at her clinic, who invited her to attend a reformed synagogue with her later in the week. Although Judith was grateful for the loving attention the chaplain lavished upon her, she believed (as she had been taught) that Reformed Jews were only pretending to be Jewish and were also cut off from the inheritance of Israel. Although at the synagogue she might have found community, support, and a new understanding of what it meant to be Jewish, she could not shake her formative paradigm, could not reach out and take the help offered to her because those desiring to help were, like she believed of herself, "not Jewish enough."

Thus Jack Believers' alienation is often enforced by their own families, and because they are "trapped" within the belief system, they cannot free themselves from their toxic effects. Because Judith did not believe that another system could be pleasing to God, she had to somehow resign herself to banishment from the divine presence.

Meaning

Again, the Jack Believer's ability to find meaning in his or her life can only be properly described in negative terms. There is no positive meaning to one's life. Positive meaning is only found by following the straight-and-narrow proscriptions of the Traditional community, and since the Jack Believer clearly falls outside of this locus of grace, no positive meaning can be appropriated. Jack Believers measure their lives by what they cannot have, and are therefore often self-destructive, turning to temporary means of solace invariably condemned by their own worldview such as alcohol, drugs, and promiscuous sexual behavior.

Tango is a Muslim driven from his family for being a homosexual. He subsisted on the street in San Francisco for three years, working in the sex trade, but eventually, with the assistance of a concerned sugar daddy, was able to complete high school and went to trade school to be a cook. He has his own apartment now, and a steady job. He still feels damned and rejected by both his family and Allah, and the pain of it is almost overwhelming. He did not choose to be gay and could not "fake" a happy married life as his parents pressured him to do. To stifle the pain, he goes to the gay bars south of Market Street. Any time not spent at work is usually consumed swilling beer and chasing tail.

Both of these activities—drinking and promiscuous sex—reinforce his feeling of alienation, but they also numb the pain and provide distractions—a never-ending viscious circle. Tango is typical of many Jacks. The next drink or the next sexual encounter may not have any transcendent purpose, but it is, at least, a reason to go on living.

The only exception to this is for those who, driven by their anger at the injustice aimed at them from their faith community, actively seek to undermine the community. For those coming from a Christian culture, it can take the form of embracing Satanism or some other occult path condemned by the Traditional community. Although only a minority of Jack Believers go this far, it can be experienced as a real liberation, and indeed salvation, for those who do, even if it is only a temporary and earth-bound salvation. Since they believe they are damned already (and at this point the notion that there may be degrees of damnation is unimportant), "going to the dark side" can reorient the Jack Believer's life in what feels like authentically positive directions. It affords them a supportive community (made up in part of other Jacks), a workable path of spiritual growth (more on this below), and gives their lives meaning. This meaning is largely oriented around revenge against the deity and the community that has condemned the Jack Believer, which, although pretty negative, at least provides a sense of purpose.

Sources of Spiritual Wisdom

Jack Believers honor the same sources of wisdom as their Traditional communities, but usually do not consult them as doing so often brings with it feelings of shame and alienation. In addition, because they are so fixated on those parts of the scriptures that condemn them, they cannot appropriate any of the positive messages that the scriptures have to offer.

Ellen was raised in a strict Lutheran home and was well-trained in the Hebrew and Christian scriptures. She won every Bible drill as a child in Sunday school, able to locate passages at lightening speed, often reading to the end of the passage while her competitors were still flipping pages. In her late teens, Ellen discovered she was pregnant. She was just about to leave for a prestigious Lutheran college, and she saw her life grinding to an ignoble halt. So, without consulting her parents, she had an abortion. She thought everything would go back to normal after that, but she was wrong. She could not forgive herself for what she considered to be a most horrible sin.

Again and again she read the Mosaic punishments for those who take the life of an innocent. Her guilt consumed her, and she eventually dropped out of college due to failing grades. The campus chaplain tried to intervene, and without divining the cause of her guilt, saw her intense scrupulosity and self-directed rage as being similar to Martin Luther's. He pointed out to her that she and Luther were similar, and if he could find peace with God, so could she. He pointed out the passages from the apostle Paul that had been so moving for Luther himself, but she was not budging. "Martin Luther never killed his baby," she thought to herself, arms folded in protection, waiting for the chaplain to tire of his sermon and simply go away.

Life did not get any easier for Ellen after that. But she did manage to navigate a meaningful existence working as a travel agent. She has not yet returned to church and does not even own a Bible. Like Ellen, many Jack Believers may eventually come to view their own existence and experience in positive terms, though they will probably not universalize these sources; they remain firmly in the "works for me" category.

Spiritual Growth

Jacks accept the same model of spiritual growth as Traditional Believers, the submission of one's own will to that of the Divine. But the Jacks are those who have not submitted their will, or cannot. Spiritual growth is assessed, once again, in negative terms, in how far one has removed oneself from the divine will.

The exceptions, once again, are those who have embraced their rebellion, such as Satanists. This provides a subsystem resident within the Traditional paradigm, where a whole new schema of spiritual growth is offered, usually a complex system of occult initiations that personally empower the Jack Believer in open defiance of the deity. Though they believe this salvation is temporary and that their damnation will one day be at hand, in the short term this new system can provide salvific elements such as community, self-empowerment, self-esteem, and mystical union with spiritual (albeit demonic) powers.

Griffin was raised in a Seventh-Day Adventist home and was heavily involved in his youth group in junior high. When both of his parents died in a car accident, he was moved into foster care with a non-Adventist family. He felt as if God had turned his back on him, so he turned his own back as a result. His foster parents had a parenting style that clashed with what he had known, and the conflict drove him to withdraw. He felt rejected and disempowered, and, barely graduating high school, he went to work in construction.

The influence of his co-workers was a mixed blessing. He had a social life again, but he also had abandoned his Adventist prohibitions against meat, alcohol, and drugs. When one of his co-workers invited him to "a cool ritual with a naked woman on the altar," he couldn't resist. He found himself at a Black Mass performed by a local branch of the Church of Satan. He loved the horror-show aesthetics and the air of sexual excitement that rippled through him during the ritual. He went back the next week, and before long was a regular fixture.

To his surprise, he discovered many aspects of his old church life that he had forgotten he loved: regular ritual, friendship and community, and a sense of common (though admittedly dark) purpose. He liked the active rebellion being a part of the church inspired in him, and likewise enjoyed the feeling of rage at God that sometimes bubbled up in him during Mass. One time he nearly blacked out from hyperventilation.

After a while, however, though he appreciated the community, the novelty quickly wore thin. The Church of Satan is, in occult circles, not taken terribly seriously. The shocking, horrific aspects of their ritual is pretty much the point of the whole affair, and Griffin found himself wanting something more. He longed for the feeling of connection that he used to enjoy as a child. Secretly admitting this to a fellow worshipper, he forgot about it until he received a phone call a couple of days later. His friend had invited him to a meeting of the Lodge of the Hawk and Serpent, a breakaway group that took their occultism more seriously than the Church of Satan folks did.

Griffin instantly felt right at home. The Serpentines were more intellectually focused and had a much more elaborate and consistent system of magick worked out. In this environment he was able to appropriate all the benefits of a worshipping community, and also was able to avail himself of an impressive mystical system that fed him as well as satisfying his sense of rebellion. The outsider status of the Serpentines was very much congruent with his own sense of alienation. Say what you will about their ultimate purpose, in the Lodge of the Hawk and Serpent Griffin found a spirituality that embraced him where he was and met the great majority of his spiritual needs.

It must be noted that not all Satanists or occultists are Jack Believers. If Griffin stays with the Serpentines, in fact, he may find himself migrating to another point on the wheel, as Serpentine theology is not set up in opposition to the Christian pantheon the way the Church of Satan is. The shift to a more "serious" occult path may have actually been a good move for Griffin, since if he truly internalizes its teachings, he may be able to leave the baggage of his childhood wounding behind, and embrace a much more positive, if still alternative, spiritual path.

In fact, there are those on occult paths that have a very positive orientation toward Divinity (most occultists are not Satanists, after all). There are followers of occult paths represented in every faith style right around the wheel, from Traditional Believers (and yes, there *are* fundamentalist Wiccans) to Religious Agnostics. Only those occultists who embrace an intentionally negative path and truly live within the paradigm of the Traditional Believers can be counted as Jack Believers.

Practices, Advantages, and Disadvantages

There are no positive practices employed by Jack Believers. The most common activities have already been noted: alcohol abuse, drug use, and sexual promiscuity are the chief activities most found in those of this orientation. Avoidance of family members and others of one's spiritual community of origin is also common.

There are no advantages to being a Jack Believer. The best that can be said is that a Jack Believer may free him- or herself from a Traditional lifestyle that feels restrictive or unnatural to him or her, since the internal violence wrought by such a belief system is hardly worth it.

The disadvantages are many: the alienation from one's family or spiritual community, not to mention estrangement from the Divine; the dreadful lack of self-esteem, and the resulting self-destructive behavior add up to a way of life not to be recommended to anyone. Jack Believers are to be universally pitied.

Conclusion of Case

At the end of an hour, Russell felt every bit as depressed as Marsha was. He longed to give her a word of comfort or a way out of her self-imposed prison, but he despaired. He thought of Plato's parable of the cave; he could tell Marsha that there was a whole world outside—where the sun was shining and she could be free, but she was helplessly chained to the walls of the cave by her own beliefs.

She looked at her watch and started to gather her things, "Well, my flight's up soon. Thanks for the shoulder."

"Thank you," he told her, and inwardly panicked, wanting to leave her with some word of hope. He caught her elbow and struggled for the right words. He looked her in the eye as she hesitated. "I think you deserve to be loved," he finally said, cringing at how inadequate it sounded.

"I think you've had too much wine," she said, but smiled at him. She kissed him on the cheek and was gone.

Jack Believers At-a-Glance

1. *How is the Divine imaged?* Primarily as the angry judge.
2. *What is the nature of one's relationship with the Divine?* Estrangement.
3. *How does one construct meaning in the world?* Only in negative terms.
4. *What are the accepted sources of spiritual wisdom?* Same as Traditional Believers, but cannot appropriate their benefits.
5. *How is spiritual growth assessed?* By degree of estrangement.
6. *Practices?* No positive practices are common.
7. *Advantages?* None.
8. *Disadvantages?* Low self-esteem and self-destructive behavior.

The Faith Styles Wheel

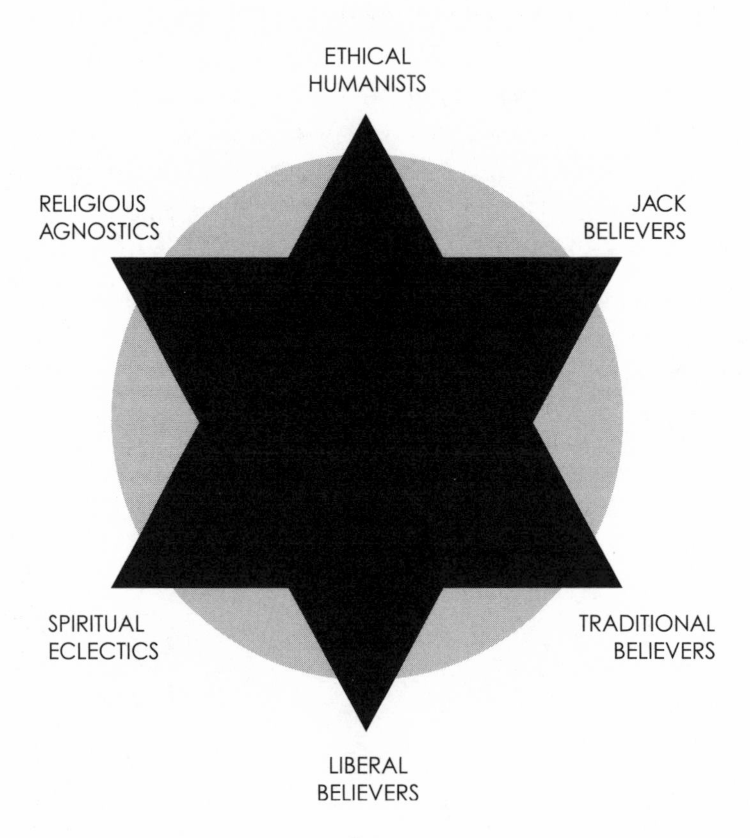

FIGURE 3: THE FAITH STYLES WHEEL

7

Companioning around the Circle

The Faith Styles system can help us understand our clients better, and thereby be better companions to them. But it can also help us understand ourselves better; specifically, it can help us determine whom we can and cannot companion effectively. It is important for us, as spiritual guides, to recognize not only our strengths, but also our limitations. In this chapter, we will consider each of the styles in reference to the spiritual guide and ask, "Which styles can companion which styles?" Some styles will be viable guides for other styles, while some are not. Awareness of our strengths and limitations will help us avoid uncomfortable and potentially damaging spiritual guidance relationships. As always, my comments on this are generalizations; there will always be exceptions.

Traditional Believers

Traditional Believers are the most limited in whom they can offer guidance to. Because the Traditional orientation is typically very clear about what is the right way and which the wrong way to approach Divinity, they will have a hard time effectively companioning people of other styles. Theirs will be the greatest temptation to mold the client in their own image. Therefore, Traditional Believers will be most effective companioning other Traditional Believers, usually those who belong to the same religious tradition. For instance, a guide who belongs to the Assembly of God denomination of Christian evangelicalism will be most effective companioning other Christian Evangelicals.

Traditional Believers are the only style that is limited to their own specific religious tradition. A Traditional Christian companioning a Traditional Hindu is most likely to fail, as few Traditional Christians could (or would ethically be able to) companion a Hindu without attempting to convert him or her. Such attempts are, in the world of spiritual guidance, nothing short of spiritual violence, and doomed to disaster.

Traditional Believers Guiding Liberal Believers. A Traditional Believer is not specifically limited to their own style, however. They may have some success with their neighbors on the wheel, with qualifications. A Traditional Believer may be able to companion a Liberal Believer, if the Liberal is not *too* Liberal. In this case, the Traditional guide and the Liberal client will need to communicate clearly about goals and expectations. If both are "on the same page," and the client is comfortable with Traditional language and theological constructs, this could be an effective pair. The guide, however, must be open to the fact that the Divine manifests differently to different people. The more open to Mystery the guide is, the greater his or her chances for success with a Liberal client.

Traditional Believers Guiding Jack Believers. A Traditional Believer may also be an extremely effective guide for Jack Believers—perhaps more so than any other style on the wheel. Since the Jack Believer shares the same theological assumptions as the Traditional Believer, they can speak the same language and agree upon the goals that are important in a given system. (Again, this only works if the guide and client are from the same—or very similar—religious traditions.) A Traditional guide who can hold out to the Jack Believer the acceptance and grace offered in their shared system with compassion rather than judgment can quite literally extend to them salvation.

Unfortunately, as we have said, Jack Believers rarely come for spiritual guidance. However, because families and extended families of Traditional Believers often contain Jacks, there is no shortage of opportunity for Traditional Believers and Jacks to share casual conversations on spiritual subjects.

Since they often still move in similar circles—and are often found together in work situations—sensitive Traditional Believers will also find frequent opportunities to minister to Jacks. The trick for Traditional Believers will be to extend love and grace to Jacks without prematurely burdening them with the moral codes they already know so well, and which only serve to alienate them from the Traditional "fold."

Liberal Believers

While Traditional Believers' ability to companion other styles extends to one point on either side of the circle, Liberal Believers' ability extends two. Liberal Believers will, of course, be most effective when companioning other Liberal Believers. But they will also find success with Traditional Believers, Jack Believers, Spiritual Eclectics, and Religious Agnostics. As far as spiritual guidance is concerned, Liberals are among the most versatile and viable of any of the faith styles.

Liberal Believers Guiding Traditional Believers. Because they are firmly grounded in a religious tradition, Liberals will be able to walk effectively with Traditional Believers of the same tradition. If a Liberal guide is appropriately reticent about his or her own self-disclosure, the Traditional client may not even be aware that he or she is not also a Traditional Believer. There is no reason to dissuade them from this assumption. Since a Liberal Believer will know the theology, vocabulary, and iconography of the tradition they share with their Traditional clients, he or she will most likely be able to meet the client where he or she is, and will be able to respect the boundaries traditionally held by the faith.

The advantage that a Liberal guide has over a Traditional guide when companioning a Traditional Believer is his or her openness to Mystery, to ways of relating to or understanding the Divine that are "outside of the box" of a given tradition. Since the Divine is rarely a tame animal, Liberal guides can help Traditional Believers weather spiritual emergencies that seem to contradict or threaten the Traditional paradigm.

The danger for Liberal guides working with Traditional clients is knowing how far is too far to stretch beyond the Traditional envelope. Since most good spiritual guidance pushes people beyond their comfort zones, this can be a tricky tightrope walk. Liberal guides must be careful not to challenge the Traditional worldview, but be willing instead to work creatively within it.

Liberal Believers Guiding Jack Believers. Liberals can be a revelation to Jack Believers, for they can show them a face of their religion unmarred by the severity and judgmentalism that drove them from the Traditional camp in the first place. While Traditional Believers feel it imperative to hold the Divine's justice and mercy in tandem, Liberal Believers are more content to emphasize mercy and regard the justice part as almost an afterthought. Traditional Believers often feel that if they do not give the carrot and stick of mercy and justice equal emphasis, they are doing their clients a disservice. Liberals, however, recognize that people who have been wounded by the stick have had quite enough of it. The carrot is sufficient lure.

Jack Believers can see in Liberals an example of forgiveness, love, and tolerance that they may never have experienced from a person of faith before. It may confound and frighten them—for since here is a person of faith who is willing to embrace them, and what's more, model the Divine's own unconditional acceptance, the only thing standing in the way of divine communion is the shame and self-loathing of the Jack him- or herself. "As long as my community rejects me, my own self-rejection can be justified," a Jack may reason, "but if this person of faith is willing to accept me, if it is true that God is willing to accept me, then what am I to do with my own disgrace?" Working through this question is the challenge for Jacks guided by Liberal Believers.

Just as in working with Traditional Believers, Liberals must be careful not to tip their hand too much to Jacks. If the Jack Believer perceives that a guide strays too far from her tradition of origin, she is likely to perceive the guide as just another backslider like herself and not possessed of any real spiritual wisdom. The tightrope walk here is to stay firmly within the boundaries of a tradition, while emphasizing the mercy inherent within it.

Liberal Believers Guiding Spiritual Eclectics. Liberal Believers and Spiritual Eclectics are often a happy mix. Eclectics frequently delight and challenge Liberals with their free-wheeling spiritual appropriations. This can sometimes be unsettling for Liberals, who are suspicious of the efficacy of a spiritual path that is not well-grounded in tradition. Liberals can help Eclectics enormously not by insisting that they put down roots (an often impossible task for Eclectics), but by providing a frequent reality check, reminding Eclectic clients to think critically and to carefully weigh evidence in their spiritual discernments.

Eclectic clients can be a real blessing to Liberals by stretching their spiritual envelopes. It is clear to Liberals that their Eclectic clients have real and vibrant relationships with the Divine, but the lengths to which they go, the weirdness of their potpourri faith can sometimes feel threatening and scary. Most Liberals rightly perceive this as their own issue, however, not their clients,' and remain open to whatever crazy dance Divinity and their client might be doing next.

Liberal Believers Guiding Spiritual Agnostics. Liberals will have a similar experience working with clients who are Spiritual Agnostics. Though they usually do not experience the same dramatic shifts in religious perspective as Eclectics, Agnostics will stretch their Liberal guides just as much. Agnostics will force Liberals to confront their own existential anxieties head on, without the shield of faith. Unless they are willing to endure this extremely uncomfortable perspective, Liberals cannot be effective guides for Agnostics. But if they can hang on tight to their own faith, Liberals can feel safe enough to venture out onto the strange and scary territory that Religious Agnostics call home—an experience meaningful and healing to both the Liberal guide and the Agnostic client.

Though free to draw insights from their faith traditions, Liberals cannot appeal to faith in working with Agnostics, at least not as conventionally understood. Faith defined as the *willed and irrational suspension of disbelief* before the apparently meaningless cosmos is something Agnostics might be willing to explore. Faith as *belief in the goodness and love of Divinity*, generally, is not. Belief is always suspect for Agnostics—a rare allergy incomprehensible to most other styles. Skepticism is the fuel that drives this particular spiritual engine, and Liberal guides will be much more effective working *with* this reticence than battling against it.

Spiritual Eclectics

Spiritual Eclectics Guiding Liberal Believers. Spiritual Eclectics often make great guides for Liberal Believers. The Eclectic appreciates the spiritual generosity of the Liberal, and at the same time envies the Liberal's rootedness in tradition, ease in the articulation of their faith, and strong spiritual community. Eclectics will enjoy working with Liberals to share in these positives vicariously. Having clients rooted in tradition and community may be as close to actually *being* so rooted as some Eclectics want to be, but even so these things will have a positive impact on an Eclectic spiritual guide.

Eclectics who are new to spiritual guidance must be careful to remember that Liberals are not Traditional Believers and hold their faith very differently. Eclectics that are too wounded by their traditions of origin may or may not be able to work with clients from that tradition. While working with Traditional Believers from such a tradition may be too painful and challenging, working with a Liberal Believer from the same tradition may be deeply healing for the Eclectic, as the Liberal may have opportunity to model a different way of holding the tradition that the guide has not seen before.

Likewise, the Eclectic guide may be a positive influence on Liberal Believers, as their wide-ranging knowledge of spiritual subjects will both support and positively challenge the Liberal's path. Eclectics will always stretch the Liberal envelope, can help Liberals think more creatively then they might feel they have license to, and can see their way around spiritual roadblocks before which Liberals sometimes feel immobilized.

Spiritual Eclectics Guiding Religious Agnostics. Eclectics will also be happy guides for Agnostics, if they can sit with the existential discomfort that fuels the Agnostic path. This will be hard for many Eclectics, whose penchant for "sweetness and light" in their spirituality is a not-unwarranted cliché. Conversely, an Eclectic's persistent spiritual optimism cannot help but to positively influence Agnostics, even if it is initially confounding. The Agnostic is likely to initially think of his or her guide as too "woo-woo" to be of any real use to them, but the openness of the Eclectic worldview to the peculiarities of the Agnostic path will not go unnoticed by the client, and can actually come as a welcome relief. Eclectics and Agnostics can form an invincible team, with Eclectics holding the faith and Agnostics holding the doubt. The interplay of this yang and yin will be beneficial to both client and guide.

Spiritual Eclectics Guiding Ethical Humanists. In the same way, Eclectics can be effective guides for Ethical Humanists. The nonjudgment with which

Eclectics can hold all spiritual perspectives is easily extended to those who have none. In fact, such a match may turn out to be an exciting new spiritual exploration for Eclectics, who are able to add the nature mysticism inherent in Humanist spirituality to their own collection of meaningful spiritual perspectives.

Humanists may initially hold the worldview of Eclectics with some disdain, but again, as with Agnostics, the optimism and flexibility of the Eclectic path will win out. The Eclectic must resist the temptation to instill faith in the Humanist, and the Humanist must resist the temptation to convince the Eclectic of the silliness of spiritual phenomena. Just as every style must remember that proselytation is forbidden, Eclectics and Humanists may need to be reminded because theirs does not look like the standard brand of proselytation. Eclectics must meet Humanists on their own ground and not break the "rules" by appealing to spiritual "realities."

Religious Agnostics

Agnostic guides must find themselves firmly rooted in a positive relationship with Mystery to be effective guides to people of more "substantive" faith than their own. An acknowledgement of ignorance as to what the Mystery may be up to is imperative, and the Agnostic guide's willed-suspension-of-disbelief muscle must be well-exercised and ready to spring into action at a moment's notice.

Religious Agnostics Guiding Liberal Believers. Although a counterintuitive match, this often has surprising and positive results, especially when the Liberal and Agnostic belong to the same religious tradition. Such Agnostics can hold a critical mirror to the faith that Liberals would often rather avoid, but which is almost always useful. Agnostics are mindful of the benefits of tradition and community—indeed it is these very factors that keep them involved in their traditions—and easily validate these things for Liberals, who can tend toward ambivalence in their commitments.

Religious Agnostics Guiding Spiritual Eclectics. This is one of the most beneficial of matches, as there are often a lot of cultural touchpoints between these two styles. Indeed, at times it can be hard to distinguish one from the other in casual conversation. The Agnostic's openness to wide-ranging spiritual wisdom is easily mistaken for eclecticism, while the Spiritual Eclectic's ability to juggle mutually exclusive worldviews can seem to some a rejection of all coherent paradigms. Religious Agnostics can be very useful guides indeed, as they often serve as "bullshit detectors" for Eclectics and can help them think critically about their sources of spiritual wisdom and religious leaders. Agnostics must be careful, however, not to be dismissive of wisdom they consider specious, which nonetheless may have great value for the Eclectic. Religious Agnostics can also be valuable models for Eclectics, bearing witness to the importance of groundedness in tradition and community.

Religious Agnostics Guiding Ethical Humanists. Another good match, Religious Agnostics may very well end up guiding other agnostics, albeit of the Humanist variety. Much more than any other style, Religious Agnostics understand the ground rules laid down by Ethical Humanists. They are less likely than other styles to have a "faith agenda," even an unconscious one, and are open to the Humanist search for truth without recourse to revelation. Understanding the importance of community, Religious Agnostics can remind Humanists that the "Lone Ranger" approach has limited efficacy, and that their aims are better served when they work in concert with others.

Religious Agnostics Guiding Jack Believers. An unlikely match if there ever was one, Religious Agnostics have almost nothing to offer Jacks. Their way of holding scripture and traditions seem indistinguishable from apostasy to Jacks—an apostasy worse than their own, in fact, since the Agnostic maddeningly refuses to admit he or she is a "backslider" and inexplicably thinks of him- or herself as part of the "fold." There is simply no category in the Jack Believer's universe to place Religious Agnostics, so they are most likely to collapse them in with themselves. They will consider Religious Agnostics to be simply other fallen-away believers who are in denial about their apostasy. Fruitless arguing will not remedy this situation.

There is, however, the possibility that, like Liberal Believers, the Religious Agnostic can model a way of holding tradition that may come as a revelation to Jack Believers. They are most likely to distrust this orientation, but with prolonged exposure (which is most likely if the Religious Agnostic is a friend, co-worker, or family member of the Jack, since few Jacks ever enter formal spiritual guidance), they may begin to see the Religious Agnostic as anomalous, which is a valuable opening. Agnostics can influence Jacks more by being living examples of faithfulness than by argument. If a Religious Agnostic can put a Traditional Believer to shame with his or her commitment to tradition, community, and philanthropy, a Jack Believer may well sit up and take notice. Though this notice is more akin to the interest one might take in a dog that can walk upright on a giant rubber ball while balancing a bone on his nose, it is notice all the same, and may in fact have a positive effect on the Jack by cracking open his or her worldview, if even only slightly.

Ethical Humanists

Unfortunately, there are few Ethical Humanists training as spiritual guides, for obvious reasons. If we widen our understanding of spiritual guidance beyond the immediately visible spiritual guidance community, however, we will see that Ethical Humanists are already training as social workers, therapists, life and values coaches, and in the Unitarian Universalist denomination, as ministers and religious educators.

Ethical Humanists Guiding Spiritual Eclectics. This can be a very good match, but only for the Humanist who can resist the sometimes overwhelming urge to poke fun at spirituality and religion. The Spiritual Eclectic already suffers a bit of a spiritual inferiority complex, since their variety of faith is not widely respected outside of their own circles. In fact, it is often openly and mercilessly ridiculed—by Humanists as often as by Traditional Believers. Humanist guides must be careful to respect the spiritual path Eclectics follow, willingly suspending their disbelief in the service of the client, trusting that the Eclectic will find a way that works for him or her, even if it seems right bloody nonsense to the Humanist. This can be hard work for some Humanists, and indeed, for some, impossible. If a Humanist guide can do this effectively, however, he or she can affirm the ecological imperative shared by both styles and help Eclectics ground their practice in activism and service.

Ethical Humanists Guiding Religious Agnostics. A common match in Unitarian Universalist circles, Humanists who find themselves guiding Religious Agnostics can be very helpful indeed by providing concrete examples of how the Agnostic's lived spirituality makes a real difference in the world. Religious Agnostics are plagued by doubt and anxiety, but the Humanist can ground this negative energy in experience and results, mostly through an emphasis on service. Humanists must be careful not to exacerbate the Agnostic tendency to doubt themselves at every turn; building confidence and trust in the universe is of paramount importance for Religious Agnostics, and Humanist guides will do well to remember the needs of their clients in this regard. Once again, it is a lot of fun to poke holes in religious tradition, and it will be hard for Humanists to resist this temptation completely, but the Religious Agnostic has already done this *ad nauseum* him- or herself and needs their admirable commitment to tradition and community affirmed rather than denigrated.

Ethical Humanists Guiding Jack Believers. Jack Believers are literally between a rock and a hard place. Their options are very limited indeed: conform to the Traditional paradigm or prepare for damnation (and for many, damnation is already an all-too-present reality). There is another way out, however, that many Jacks have availed themselves of—the eschewing of religion altogether. It is only human for people to say to themselves, "Well, if God is going to reject me, I'm going to reject God." For some, this takes the form of anti-God religion (such as Satanism), but for many more, it is the eschewing of religion altogether.

This is a tricky transition, which we will focus on more in the next chapter. Suffice it to say here that the Humanist can companion the Jack by holding out the promise that there is life *after* religion—that real meaning can be found, as well as real purpose. Humanists can serve as invaluable role models for Jacks, demonstrating for them that once the monster-deity has been slain, the universe does not disintegrate, nor are they thrown into hell. This will be a time of very high anxiety for Jacks, and Humanists who can hold this journey with compassion and tenderness can offer a more real salvation to Jack Believers than Jacks have ever experienced before.

8

Migration around the Circle

Most spiritual guides would agree that trying to "convert" a client from one faith style to another is a form of spiritual violence and is always abhorrent. This kind of spiritual arrogance is almost always harmful to the client and has no place in spiritual guidance or ministry. However, it is not uncommon for a client to instigate such transition themselves. This can be a time of scary revelation or exhilarating epiphanies, and either way the companionship of a soul friend can be very helpful to ground, guide, and normalize the client's experience.

Many things can precipitate the migration from one point on the circle to another—serious illness, grief, unprecedented life experiences, spiritual epiphanies, exposure to other cultures and beliefs, or simply the curiosity and growth that is a normal part of human living. Whatever the catalyst, it is our duty as spiritual guides to give the Divine the benefit of the doubt—that the Divine knows what it is doing and that such migration is in the service of the health and wholeness of the client. The shift from one point to another may be an exploratory phase, it may be a life change, or it may simply be a temporary resting point on the way to another point on the wheel.

It is my experience that migration occurs around the wheel in one direction or another to adjacent points. While many religious traditions uphold the idea that conversion can happen from any place and walk of life to their own point (usually these are Traditional Believers), other traditions hold that conversion is almost always a slow and incremental process, and announcements of "conversion" may seem instantaneous, but actually occur only when the transition is complete and comfortable enough to publicly embrace. This latter model is the understanding according to which this chapter will proceed. Clients may indeed continue to migrate to far points on the wheel, but these shifts will most often be made incrementally, that is, leaping from one adjacent point to another. For instance, a Religious Agnostic may indeed eventually embrace an identity as a Liberal Believer, but is most likely to move through a period as a Spiritual Eclectic first.

In this chapter we will look at some examples of people journeying from one point on the circle to another, addressing some of the issues involved, and offering what I hope will be some useful suggestions to those accompanying them.

Traditional Believers

Traditional Believer to Liberal Believer. When Margaret first started working at the homeless shelter, she did so out of a sense of divine calling. A conservative Roman Catholic, she was a little unnerved to discover that a portion of the population she would be serving were Muslims. The first night the Safi family showed up at her shelter, she found herself profoundly moved by the hardship they had faced, especially since the terrorist attacks. Mr. Safi had experienced much difficulty finding steady work, and the children had been persecuted in the public schools. Mrs. Safi had asked her if she would pray for them, and, taken aback, she surprised herself by saying that yes, of course, she would. One night, she walked past their cots to discover Mrs. Safi praying over a string of beads that looked all the world to her like a rosary. When Mrs. Safi had finished, Margaret asked her about it. The prayers were different, but the similarities unnerved her.

Margaret's heart broke for them, and she took this pain to her spiritual guide at their next session. It occurred to her that God must feel even more compassion for them than she did, that God loved them utterly and must regard them as faithful people. Margaret's spiritual director pointed out to her that the Vatican II documents explicitly declared that the Catholic Church rejects no truth found in other religions, but indeed embraces and celebrates it.

Gradually, Margaret found a new way of holding her own faith. She began to think of Catholicism as right for her, and Islam as right for the Safi family. This allowed her to soften even more towards them, to see them as human beings rather than "non-believers." Eventually, when Mrs. Safi invited Margaret to attend their mosque with them, she was touched and felt honored, even if she was not yet ready to accept her offer. Her spiritual guide pointed out that not long ago she would have been horrified or even offended by the suggestion. At that point Margaret had to acknowledge that her faith had shifted, and that she was no longer as certain about many things as she once was, and that this uncertainty felt spacious and liberating rather than scary.

Like Margaret, many Traditional Believers have life experiences that cause them to question the absolute claims made by their traditions. Face to face with some ambiguity or incongruity, the "center" no longer "holds," and they find they must reevaluate often long-held beliefs. Perhaps this is exposure to people of other faiths, like Margaret; for some it might be the outing of a gay or lesbian son or daughter. For those who are of a thoughtful bent, it may simply be that the contradictions inherent in Traditional Belief may simply become too arduous to sustain, and a new way of holding one's faith tradition must be sought.

Those in transition from Traditional Belief to Liberal Belief will typically experience a great deal of anxiety. Spiritual guides will serve clients well by reassuring them that the Divine will not punish them for thinking the thoughts that are occurring to them, and by being encouraging and supportive whenever their ideas and feelings venture outside of the Traditional "box."

This migration will often necessitate a change of worshipping communities, though this is not always the case. Margaret's spiritual guide happens to know that the associate priest at Margaret's parish is a Liberal Believer himself, and may recommend that she pay him a visit. If she does, Fr. Dave can steer her to many parish ministries and activities that can support her new growth. Others, however, may need to leave their Traditional communities behind in favor of another that has a more Liberal spiritual orientation. Often this can be done within the same denomination, although in the case of some, such as in Judaism, it may entail switching denominations (there are no Liberal Orthodox Jewish synagogues, for instance, but a Conservative Synagogue may be just the thing).

Such a switch may be more traumatic than the change in thinking, since one's congregation is often a person's chief source of community and validation. Those exchanging a Traditional belief system for a Liberal orientation may find leaving their communities of origin painful at best. Often family members and close friends are part of the Traditional community and may actively shun the client in transition. When this is the case, spiritual guides would do well to suggest more frequent meetings to provide adequate support for the transition. Clients should be encouraged to seek support in Liberal communities as soon as possible and may need a period of separation from family and Traditional friends until they feel secure enough in their new orientation to withstand the sometimes oppressive resistance they may experience.

It must be said that Traditional friends and relatives do not mean to be oppressive. They truly believe that the client is "going astray" and may be eternally endangering their souls in their new explorations. There is genuine concern and grief to contend with in those "left behind," and spiritual guides in some communities may find themselves playing both sides of the fence, especially if they have clients belonging to both camps. In such cases, it is important for spiritual guides to remember that there is no agenda beyond what the Divine is doing in their midst, to avoid dehumanizing anyone—regardless of their faith orientation—and help both parties to adjust to the transition in ways that diminish alienation and promote community and communication. Since there is an increasing bias in the spiritual guidance community against Traditional Belief, appropriate care for such Believers cannot be overemphasized.

Traditional Believer to Jack Believer. Raised in a Greek Orthodox home, Demetri knew he was different even as a young child. Throughout his childhood, he was an active member of his church's youth group and successfully hid the fact that he really felt like a girl inside. By the time he was in his midteens, however, his hormones kicked into high gear, and he was unable to deny or hide his true identity.

He secretly renamed himself Demi, but when she admitted to those she loved that she thought she was born the wrong gender, her priest declared her *anathema*, and her father threw her out of her home. She internalized these messages and believed that she was indeed damned, though not through any fault of her own. She was clear that she did not choose to be female and could not deny her feelings, but she also believed the teachings of her church.

With the proper modeling and encouragement, Demi might have found her way to a Liberal Believer orientation, become involved in an Episcopal Church or some other liturgical community that provided some continuity with her heritage, yet could also support her full humanity as a transgendered person. But Demi did not find that kind of support; instead she found herself on the street, begging and turning tricks to stay alive. She quickly found that alcohol and heroin numbed the deep pain and self-loathing she felt.

People such as Demi are not easy to help. The contradiction between who they are and who they feel they should be is often overwhelming and drives many to despair and self-distruction, whether quick or slow. Since Demi is unlikely to seek spiritual guidance in any formal sense, the Divine may need to employ other means to reach her. It may be that a compassionate individual at the Harm Reduction Center can show her that it is possible for a transgendered person to have a positive and affirming spiritual life. The street priests from the Old Catholic Needle Exchange may show her that there are catholic clergy who do not reject or hate her. Anything that can offer Demi another way of holding her faith—and therefore herself—and to restore her self-image as being amongst God's beloved will be of help.

Liberal Believers

Liberal Believer to Traditional Believer. A year ago Rachel was in an automobile accident that left her with a concussion and limited use of her left arm. She was fortunate—her son Jacob was killed in the same accident. A year of physical therapy had restored much of the use of her hand, but there was no repairing her heart.

She didn't blame the other driver, or God, but she did blame herself. Even though Jacob had been driving at the time, it was on an errand for her that the tragedy occurred, and she could not forgive herself. An active member of her Reformed Synagogue ever since her divorce, she was simply inconsolable after Jacob's loss, and there was only so much her rabbi could do to help her. As her depression and grief deepened, her rabbi's visits became more infrequent—finally she stopped visiting altogether.

When the High Holy Days came around, she thought about just not going. Then a friend invited her to the Yom Kippur service at his temple. She shrugged and agreed, not realizing or caring where. When she and her friend arrived at Beth Israel, she realized with a start that it was an Orthodox synagogue. No matter, she was here, she thought, and went inside.

She was taken aback by the richness of the liturgy that day. The traditional chants brought back memories from her childhood, and for the space of a few hours she felt like a little girl again, safe in the womb of family, insulated from the harsh, cold, world. She discovered she did not want to leave and wept bitterly in the bathroom.

She did leave, but she came back, again and again. Her friend was overjoyed to have her join him for services regularly, and a romance began brewing. Rachel felt as if she had been reborn and clung to the rituals and the preaching of her new rabbi with a ferocity and hunger she had forgotten. For the first time in years, she felt as if life had order and meaning. She had a safe, ritual container in which to mourn Jacob, and a context in which to understand her loss. She went to her new rabbi for spiritual counseling and found in him a warm and sincere spirit. She joined a couple of committees and felt not only a part of a community, but at one with the great and scattered people of Israel, which took on transcendent meaning she had for years forgotten.

In spite of the objections of her inner hippie, she began to pay close attention to keeping kosher, observing Shabbat, and performing mitzvahs. One day she woke up and realized she was Orthodox. She surprised herself in that, instead of being horrified, as she might have been a couple of years ago, she felt good. She felt *home*.

Like Rachel, many people have found great solace in Traditional Belief. The ambiguities that drive Liberal Belief can, in times of crisis and sorrow, often seem hollow and meaningless. People who are frightened or suffering crave answers and security, which is Traditional Belief's stock in trade. Liberal Belief excels in offering questions, but in a world as uncertain and tempest-tossed as ours can be, Traditional Belief can be a welcome safe harbor.

Spiritual Guides who are companioning those in transition from Liberal to Traditional Belief systems must be very careful to keep their own biases in check. Those not of a Traditional Belief system are keen to rail against the prejudice and narrowness of the Traditional worldview, oblivious to their own prejudice and narrowness when it comes to Traditional Belief. Spiritual guides must take a fearless inventory of their own opinions and agendas and be careful to leave these outside of the session.

Likewise, Traditional guides must work overtime to keep their own delight in check when Liberal Believers begin to court Traditional Belief. It may be a temporary flirtation, or it may be that the Divine has something important to teach the client, but that Traditional Belief may not be the client's true home. Like all spiritual guides, Traditional professionals must exercise caution in not letting their own spiritual agendas dominate the session, as well as not projecting their own spiritual journeys onto the client.

There are many reasons why a client may transition to Traditional Belief after many years in Liberal communities. Like Rachel, it may be that the Traditional Belief system provides a sense of hope, meaning, and safety that is desperately needed by the client. Traditional Belief is very attractive to anyone who feels overwhelmed by the change and relativism that define our contemporary culture.

Spiritual guides can best assist clients migrating to Traditional Belief by keeping in mind the needs and desires that drive them. They must also keep in mind the designs of the Divine to draw the client to the bosom of the Holy and give them succor and rest. Arguing about the inconsistencies inherent in the Traditional Belief system, or railing against the perceived intolerance and oppression of such systems is not helpful to the client, and responsible guides will take their feelings to supervision to vent.

Clients transitioning to Traditional faith are usually doing so out of a deeply felt and very human need to connect with history, others, and the Divine, and to establish moral boundaries that feel safe and meaningful. These are good and healthy motivations, and spiritual guides must trust the client and the Divine and be open to the mystery play being enacted in their midst.

Liberal Believer to Spiritual Eclectic. Patul was raised in an active and liberal Hindu family. Ever since he was a small boy, his parents brought him to the ashram for weekly *puja* (devotional worship), and he was active in his small but intimate youth group.

Their guru was a kind and quiet American who had gone off to India in his early twenties to find enlightenment. Now Swami Ted led an ashram in downtown St. Paul, Minnesota, and lunched regularly with the local UUA minister and ELCA pastors. Their congregation was active in the cooperative homeless shelter and soup kitchen programs in their neighborhood, and regularly raised money to support programs for the poor back in India.

Swami Ted was surprised to receive a distressed phone call from Patul's mother, in which she complained that she had found a Catholic rosary and holy card on Patul's personal altar, among other things. He invited her to come to his office that same afternoon and tried to appear as concerned as he could. Other mothers would be reacting like this for finding condoms, marijuana, or girlie magazines under the mattress. But a rosary—how horrifying!

When she arrived, she described what she had found: the rosary and the holy card. "I also found this," she said and placed posable figurines of what appeared to be a superhero with a huge skull on his chest, and a plastic replica of a paper cup with a human face on it. "These, I have no idea what they are. They scare me."

Swami Ted stifled a chuckle and made an effort to be sympathetic. "Will you talk to him?" She pleaded. He assured her he would and told her not to worry.

He reached Patul on his cell phone and asked him if he could come by after school the next day for a mid-afternoon snack at the bagel place down the street—the bagels would be on Swami Ted. Patul agreed readily, not only because of the prospect of free bagels, but also because he was genuinely fond of Ted. When they'd ordered and received their bagels and schmears, the Swami got down to business. "Okay, don't tell your Mom I told you this, but she came to see me because she's worried about you."

Patul rolled his eyes, "What now?"

"Nothing major. She found the Catholic stuff and a couple of dolls on your altar in your bedroom, and it freaked her out a little."

"A little?" Patul teased. "Do you think? You've never invited me out for bagels by myself before. Something had to be up."

"Just between you and me," Swami Ted said, conspiratorily, "I have a Catholic picture of Jesus on my altar at home."

"I won't tell Mother," said Patul.

"Good boy," Swami Ted smiled. "I promised her I'd talk to you, though. So, here we are."

"Good bagels—thanks."

"My pleasure. I'd love to hear about what the rosary and holy card bring up for you when you see them."

"Well, I don't know how to say it. It's just a feeling. I like Jesus. He has Krishna energy."

"I know just what you mean. What about the rosary and the other stuff?"

"I like those old Madonna CDs. Don't tell the other guys in the youth group, okay? The other stuff, well, it's hard to put into words. I put those things there because of feelings. They don't make a lot of sense when you just talk about it. But when I put them there, it just . . . well, it *felt* right. Like the Punisher." Ted assumed he was talking about the superhero action figure. "I like him because he's like Kali, nobody gets in his way. He has power, you know? He does what is right no matter who tries to stop him. I want to be like that. And Master Shake . . ."

"Master Shake I know. Don't tell your Mother, but I'm a huge Aquateen Hunger Force fan."

"Dude, you are the coolest guru."

"I work overtime at that. What does Master Shake represent?"

"He's like that part of me that doesn't give a shit about anyone else."

"That's Shake, all right. Why put him on your altar? Is that something you want to encourage in yourself?"

"No, but I know he's a part of me. Better to know he's there than not to know what he's up to. You know, 'Keep your friends close and your enemies closer.'"

Swami Ted looked at him with admiration for the fine and conscious shadow work the young man was doing. "I totally get it. Where did you hear that quote?"

"Star Trek."

"That's some good spiritual teaching, there."

Patul shrugged. "It just *felt* right."

"You know, some gurus say that Jesus was an incarnation of Vishnu."

"Man, can't a guy flirt with another religion without it just turning into more Hinduism?"

Swami Ted laughed deep from his belly. He wiped his eyes, and finally said, "That, my friend, is both the advantage and liability of being a Hindu."

Swami Ted knew Patul was in no danger. He saw before him a curious teenager, and he truly admired Patul's ability to listen to and respond to his intuition and emotion. He saw in Patul's altar-making a genuine spiritual practice that, for all of its eclecticism, was deepening his sense of connection to the Divine, as well as revealing aspects of his interior world to which most teens his age were completely oblivious.

Liberal Believers may find themselves transitioning to being Spiritual Eclectics when they feel energetically drawn to spiritual teachings, mystical writings, or iconographical images not derived from their traditions of origin. This does not mean that they no longer esteem elements of their tradition, but that their scope of religious inspiration is widening to contain elements from other traditions, popular culture, and more esoteric sources.

This is an intuitive path in which the seeker literally "feels out" a new spirituality one image at a time. Like Patul, these images might suddenly appear on altars, or a person might expand into a wider range of spiritual reading, or go on an extended quest to explore other worship environments.

In all cases, spiritual guides will do well to recognize that their parishioners and clients are making conscious and deliberate attempts to connect with the Holy, even if sometimes such connections come wrapped in unlikely packages, like Patul's enshrinement of Master Shake, a highly misanthropic cartoon character from late night TV.

Spiritual guides who can honor their clients' often wide-ranging pursuit of spiritual nourishment will find that such explorations can lead to powerful and deep epiphanies, often clad in the most iconoclastic and counterintuitive clothing.

New Spiritual Eclectics may need to be reminded, as their search for new images and elements widens, not to forsake the important role of community. They may also need some encouragement to stay rooted in a sense of tradition, even if they hold it more lightly than they did before, and even while enjoying the fruit of many trees.

While Patul's explorations may take him far afield in his prayer life, Swami Ted is not concerned that he will leave the youth group anytime soon. Wisely, he also finds a way to honor both Patul's new images and encourage his continued groundedness in tradition.

"Do you perform puja at your home altar?" Swami Ted was referring to the traditional Hindu practice of waving lights in front of the images of the deities as an act of worship.

"Yeah, sometimes. I just use candles though, 'cause my Mom's afraid I'll burn the house down with the camphor."

Swami Ted laughed again. "Your Mom is wise. I hate that stuff."

"So why don't you just use candles at the ashram?"

Swami Ted put on his best Zero Mostel. "Tradition!" he thundered.

Spiritual Eclectics

Spiritual Eclectic to Liberal Believer. Maria is a third-generation Mexican-American who converted to Wicca in high school. In college she stopped practicing Wicca as a spiritual path, but still felt a spiritual connection to many of the religion's core values and symbolism. But like most Spiritual Eclectics, the snowball of her soul picked up many other images and symbols as she rolled along. Her walls at home were festooned with a veritable smorgasborg of interfaith iconography. Several pictures of her namesake, the Madonna, were in evidence, as well as statues of the Buddha, Shiva, Ganesha, and Michaelangelo's David.

Her friend Carrie had started seeing an interfaith spiritual guide about a year ago, and raved so much about her that Maria decided to give it a try, so she gave Peggy a call. Peggy was a Reconstructionist Jew, with a very open attitude toward other faiths. Right from the start Maria and Peggy hit it off, and Maria very quickly got the hang of this spiritual guidance thing.

Peggy was sympathetic to Maria's Eclectic approach to spirituality and very supportive of her many wide-ranging explorations. But she was concerned that Maria had no spiritual practices or disciplines to ground her. She suggested that Maria try meditation.

"I'm terrible at meditation," Maria complained.

"Everyone's terrible at meditation," Peggy countered.

"That's not true. I have friends that are naturals."

"Naturally tenacious, I'll wager. I understand that it's hard for you, but I'd still like you to try it, and then we can discuss what was hard, what happened during the meditation, and whatever thoughts you have about it afterward."

"Well, it'll be a good conversation starter. But I don't know what I'm doing. What do I do?"

"There's a free day of meditation at the Stillpoint Buddhist Retreat Center next month. Why don't we go together?"

Maria agreed, and the retreat day was a revelation to her. She was very grateful to Peggy for her suggestion, and she began to sit meditation daily. She began to keep a journal of the insights she gained during her meditation, and it soon became a primary source of conversation for their guidance sessions. Soon Maria was a regular fixture at Stillpoint, and she began to explore Buddhism as a serious path.

She started attending an Engaged Buddhism study group that emphasized the connection between Buddhist compassion for all beings and environmental sustainability. Before long, her meditation sessions were augmented by activism with an umbrella organization of Green Buddhists.

One day she showed up at her spiritual guidance session with a serious and surprised look on her face. "Oh my God, Peggy. I just realized I've turned into a Buddhist. When did that happen? When did I start wearing a *mala*? What happened to me?"

Peggy laughed. "Where did that old Maria go to? Do you miss her?"

"Not at all. I just really wanted to thank you for pushing me to go to that retreat day. It changed my life, and very much for the better."

"How so?" Peggy knew that it had, but she wanted to hear Maria articulate it for herself.

"Well, I have twice as many friends as I did six months ago—friends that share my values and that really care about each other and the world. I feel like I'm going deep into a spiritual life, where I was only really skating along on the surface before. You broke the ice, you know. I feel like a different person. I feel like the person I was six months ago was a fake, just a face I presented to the world, and that I pretended was me. I'm figuring out who I really am now, and that is a very different person. I feel like, before, I had all these ideas and images, but they were kind of random, there was no discernable pattern to them. Now, they're all still there, but they've all kind of clicked into place, into a logical, coherent whole. I'm not saying this very well. . . ."

"You're doing fine."

"I'm saying it's good. I'm saying thank you."

Peggy recognized that, like most Spiritual Eclectics, Maria could only go so far in her spiritual life without a spiritual discipline to ground her. Her nudging bordered on being directive, but that is appropriate sometimes, and was certainly the right thing to do in this case.

Peggy certainly wasn't intending for Maria to convert to Buddhism, she was simply encouraging her to find a spiritual practice that would support her journey without being ideologically limiting. In this way, Peggy honored Maria's Eclectic spiritual path. If Maria had embraced meditation but not Buddhism as a whole, Peggy might have next suggested ways for Maria to find community congruent with her lifestyle and spiritual orientation. But as it was, when Maria found a practice, she found a community, too.

Spiritual Eclectics are often drawn to Liberal expressions of tradition for similar reasons: Liberal Believers share many core values and ideals as Spiritual Eclectics—they are extraordinarily compatible styles. Thus, it is not a hard transition to make, and often very inviting once the Spiritual Eclectic sees what he or she has been missing.

Most Eclectics are hungry for community, and it is hard to overemphasize the importance of spiritual community to the life of the spirit. Becoming involved in a Liberal community of faith can be like coming home to Eclectics, so long as they feel free to be themselves and transition at their own pace. Spiritual guides can help clients by encouraging them to become involved for the sake of community, even if they do not completely buy into the belief system.

Tradition will provide treasures unlooked for and even unimagined by Eclectics, who typically see religious tradition in terms of fundamentalism, rigidity, and dogma. The Liberal community of faith can be a real revelation, for many have never seen that it is possible to maintain their intellectual independence and integrity and still be included in a faith community of a specific tradition. The depth of most spiritual traditions can come as a shock when their enormity and true value is finally glimpsed, and clients may need some loving containment to weather the vertigo of this revelation. Spiritual guides can also help clients sort through their projections and prejudices about a tradition, while holding up the possibility that there are other ways to hold tradition until the client can trust and invest in it.

Being grounded in a Liberal tradition does not mean that Eclectics will abandon all vestiges of their Eclectic spirituality, however. They may still have numerous images from a variety of traditions in residence on their home altars, yet their spirituality and practice can become firmly grounded in tradition and a community of faith.

This transition is almost always beneficial, as a Spiritual Eclecticism that is well-grounded and well-connected to community is both hard to find and difficult to sustain. Migration to Liberal Belief is not the ideal for all Spiritual Eclectics, but will be beneficial for many who feel the divine tug in that direction.

Spiritual Eclectic to Religious Agnostic. Troy's journey is similar to Maria's in many ways. His friends called him a "dabbler" since his spiritual life was a little bit of this, a little bit of that. In truth, he had a much greater spiritual sensibility than his friends, but because he was not dogmatic at all, what they considered his eccentric "dabbling" was not alienating. They even accompanied him sometimes to the odd Hindu temple or Gnostic mass, especially if he promised it would be "trippy." It often was.

Then tragedy struck, and Troy's best friend Rick died overnight from an aneurysm. He and the rest of his pack were devastated, and it suddenly seemed to him that all his "dabbling" was nothing but shallow spiritual tourism. When confronted by the void, he found that he didn't believe any of it, and that there was a sucking hole in his soul that he didn't know how to fill.

He had had some very positive encounters with a local Unitarian Universalist minister in his neighborhood, and when the despair over Rick's death threatened to overwhelm him, he gave her a call. Melanie had to move some appointments around, but she managed to clear some time to see him in the early afternoon. Over the period of an hour, she sat with him as he railed against God, the gods, fate, nature, and every other unseen force that may have conspired to take Rick from this plane. When he was exhausted and had asked every question he could think of, he looked her straight in the eyes and asked the last and most important one, "Why?"

Without missing a beat, Melanie said, "I don't know."

"Then what are you doing here?" he swept his arms around, indicating the church.

"Asking the same questions you are, every week, out loud," she said. "We call it worship."

"You're supposed to have answers," he accused.

"You mistake us for some other religion," she countered. "If you want answers, try the church down the street. This church is about questions—questions that don't necessarily have easy answers. The kinds of questions you're asking, now."

"Then what good is it?" He looked like he felt angry and betrayed.

"Why don't you come on Sunday and find out?"

"I've been to services here."

"Yes, as a sightseer. Why don't you bring your raw and broken heart, and all of these questions, and a good dose of that anger you're feeling. It'll make for a pretty packed pew, but I guarantee, it'll be a different experience from what you had last time."

Troy followed her guidance and showed up for worship on Sunday. She was right. The readings included one from Rilke about learning to live the questions. The songs were empty of any pie-in-the-sky platitudes, but instead filled with values that Troy already embraced. About halfway through the service, he relaxed, and all the tension just poured out of him. Then he began to cry.

A woman in her eighties, wearing a top she must have knit herself—and poorly—moved into the space next to him and put her head on his shoulder. He collapsed into her and sobbed. After the service, several people stopped him to see if he was all right, and to invite him to join them for the parish picnic at the nearby park. Even though he had plans, he blew them off and went to the picnic instead. Before long he was stuffing himself on fried chicken and Swedish tofu balls. He even joined in a game of Frisbee football. He made another appointment to speak to Rev. Melanie before he left.

At this meeting, he seemed calmer. "How are you doing?" She asked him.

"I don't know," he answered truthfully.

"Good answer," she smiled. "You'll get used to that one around here. We're not big on the 'knowing' part, but we're really good at the 'together' thing."

"I'm really surprised," he admitted. "I expected you to be like other churches—having some agenda to push. I just thought it might be a more liberal agenda than most. But you don't."

"Oh, we do," she corrected him, "it's just not about 'beliefs' as such. It's more about actions—how we treat each other is so much more important than what we believe. Beliefs come and go, change and adapt. But love, well, that never changes, does it?"

"But what do I do with this . . . not knowing? I want to fix it somehow."

"What if there's nothing to fix? Sure, you could anesthetize yourself so you don't feel the pain of that not-knowing. Or you could tell yourself a nice story that explains everything and puts it all in a nice, neat little bow, but we both know you'd be lying to yourself. So what's left? Nothing but being *with* those big, painful questions with as much courage and honesty as you can muster, supported by a community of people who have faced this kind of pain and worse, and have survived because of their love for each other."

"What do I do?"

"Just keep coming back. Let us love you. Live your questions. Don't sell out for easy answers or quick fixes. Look that void square in the face and keep asking 'why?' until you reach a place of peace."

Like many people, Troy found himself in trouble when a major existential crisis rocked his world. Without the groundedness of a spiritual tradition or community, many Spiritual Eclectics are ill-equipped to weather the storms life capriciously sends our way. It doesn't take much to tip an Eclectic whose faith is a random assemblage without root toward unbelief. Fortunately for Troy, such tipping resulted not in a complete loss of faith, but a renewal of it. In his local Unitarian Universalist minister, he found a kindly and patient spiritual guide to companion him through his dark time, and in the parish he found a community to hold and nurture him as he reoriented himself spiritually.

The Unitarian Universalist Association is a unique denomination with a high percentage of Religious Agnostics who have long known what Troy is just now discovering: that a path of rigorous intellectual inquiry does not preclude the joys and benefits of community. Of course, Religious Agnostics can be found in almost all faiths and denominations, even more traditional ones—sometimes clandestinely, sometimes openly. I fondly remember the (mostly elderly) people in many churches I have attended who swore they didn't believe a word of it, but were always there with hammer in hand on work days, and were always the first to clean the tables and do the dishes after the potluck. Like other Religious Agnostics, something prevented their whole-hearted intellectual assent to the favored dogma, but were nonetheless as involved with the community as any "true believer."

It is not always crisis that instigates such migration. Sometimes it occurs as the result of a long search for both internal integrity and external support and validation. Those two needs sum up the basic requirements for most Religious Agnostics, the two horns of the spiritual dilemma that typify their spiritual lives. Spiritual guides who can honor both can be invaluable to the difficult and fragile journeys of those Spiritual Eclectics who take this route.

Ethical Humanists

Ethical Humanists to Religious Agnostics. Marriage was the last thing Leslie had expected. At forty-five she had had two divorces and had given up on the notion of romance. Then she met Jack on a Sierra Club hike. He was quiet at first, which intrigued her, and very, very funny, which intrigued her further. After two hikes during which they were almost inseparable, she asked him out. He hemmed and hawed, but finally agreed. Then, after several awkward moments of silence, he said, "I have a confession to make."

"Tell me you're married, and you die right here, right now."

"No!" He laughed nervously. "I know you're an atheist, and I really like you, but, well, I'm a professional clergy person. I was afraid if I told you sooner, you wouldn't want . . . well, that's my experience." He stopped trying to explain and just stared at her like a very bad little boy.

Leslie was taken aback, but not as horrified as she thought she might have been. She actually felt compassion. "It must be hard to get dates."

"That's putting it mildly," he agreed.

As it turned out, Jack was an Episcopal priest, of an exceedingly liberal variety. Which is why the most unlikely thing Leslie ever would have thought possible happened—she went to church. Later that week, she told her life coach Pam about the experience.

"It was beautiful. I mean, I had all these internal resistances, but when that incense started, and the organ music, the choir . . . it was sublime. Better than going to the orchestra. I mean, I'm not in any danger of getting religion, but I was surprised how much I enjoyed it."

"What was it like seeing Jack up there?"

"*That* was weird. I remember thinking, 'I've kissed that priest.' It felt deliciously naughty. That's a Catholic upbringing for you!" She laughed.

"Are you going to go back?"

"Oh, probably. We'll see how things go between us."

Things went well. After about six months, Jack proposed, and a date was set. And, to her amazement, Leslie found that she missed church on the weeks when she didn't go. At first, she told herself she was going to church to support Jack, but then she started to feel fond of the little old ladies that tittered over the altar cloths before and after the service. And she made a couple of friends her own age as well. Before she knew it, she had said yes to serving on a committee in charge of the parish's participation in the local interfaith food bank and homeless shelter.

She told Pam about the ups and downs of her work on the committee, and in spite of herself, Pam burst out laughing.

"Okay, what? What's so funny?"

"You're serving on a church committee."

"Yeah. So?"

"Imagine yourself a year ago—what if I had told you you'd be *serving on a church committee*?"

"Oh! I see what you mean!"

"So what do you make of all the God stuff, now?"

"Well, I don't believe it in the way most of them do. I don't believe it in the way Jack does, but that doesn't really seem to matter to any of them." She looked thoughtful for a moment. "Actually, it seems like everyone there believes something different, but they all work together for some higher good. I don't think most of them believe these words they pray in a literal way. It's more symbolic, and because it's symbolic, everyone can participate. Even me. Wow. Did I just say that? I think it's true, though. I didn't get religion, Pam, but I did get church. And dammit, I like it. They're good people. They love each other. I love them. They're doing good work." She paused. "*We* are doing good work."

Until Jack came along, Leslie had no idea that there would be anything at a Christian church that might have anything at all to interest her. But once she was exposed to a healthy, active faith community, she discovered how very much it had to offer her. She found friends, opportunities to make a difference in the world, and an invitation to explore her inner world. Not long after they were married, Pam asked her, after their formal coaching session, "So, are you still an atheist?"

"I'm not sure I was ever an atheist. I think that's just a catch-all phrase that people use because they don't want to think about any of that religion stuff too much."

"But you've been thinking about it more, now? If you're not an atheist, what are you?"

"I'm an agnostic. That's like Atheism Lite, I think. I don't know if there is a god, but I don't know if there isn't a god, either. What's the sense in being dogmatic about it either way? Life is simply too mysterious to rule anything out, you know?"

Leslie's actual beliefs had not changed much since she had met Jack, but her attitude about churches and the people who attend them went through a radical shift. The migration from Ethical Humanist to Religious Agnostic is not a common one, but it does happen. Often due to some unforeseen circumstance, when people with little religious inclination are exposed to a religious community that welcomes and embraces them, and provides occasions for them to act on their core values, they can experience a shift in their opinions. Often when people are confronted with flesh and blood realities (in this case, "church people"), the stereotypes and prejudices they have clung to give way and new, more realistic—and often more positive—opinions can form.

While Pam is not trained as a spiritual guide, she is an able life coach, and helped Leslie by asking questions that helped her explore her feelings about her relationship to Jack and his church. Spiritual guides who find themselves in this situation can do the same and will be most effective when they—like Pam—are not at all attached to the outcome. Pam does not care one way or the other if Leslie gets involved at Jack's church, but she is interested, because it is real, juicy human drama. Spiritual guides must exercise the same equanimity and lack of attachment to results. If the Humanist suspects that the guide has a personal stake in what happens, it may negatively color the relationship or the client's experience. It is curiosity, not hope, that will be of most use in such cases.

After all, this is not a case of a non-religious person being converted to a form of religion, it is a case of a person with a specific style of faith embracing a similar style that meets for them a greater number of essential and very human needs. Any pressure or coercion—even a whiff of an agenda—can endanger a person's migration and prevent him or her from appropriating valuable aspects of community life that support and cultivate their full humanity.

Jack Believers

Jack Believers to Traditional Believers. Amir was raised in a traditional Sikh family, which made being a teenager in Illinois a very difficult thing indeed. Being the brownest person in his white suburban neighborhood was hard enough, but being forced to wear a *dastar* (turban), even in high school gym class, seemed to him cruel and unusual punishment. He loved his parents, he loved his temple community, but more than anything else, he wanted to be a "normal" teenager, to fit in, to have friends.

In college, things got easier. Far away from the constant oversight of his parents, Amir stopped attending temple, and after much internal wrestling, discarded his turban and got the first haircut in his life. Afterward, he found himself wandering the streets of his college town feeling the breeze in his short hair for the first time. He felt intoxicated, guilty, liberated. The whole universe was surreal for the rest of the day.

Cutting his hair became for him symbolic of many other things about his childhood from which he was cutting his ties. He started to feel that women were interested in him for the first time, and his biology classmates bought him his first beer. It was a new world.

Unfortunately, that world became a very scary place when the winter holidays rolled around and Amir realized he would have to face his family. When he stepped off the plane, he saw his family waiting for him. He walked toward them, but they did not see him. They just kept staring at the door to the boarding tube. He walked right up to them and stood nose-to-nose with his mother.

"I'm sorry . . . " she began, about to ask the rude gentleman to get out of her line of sight, but then she saw the familiar scar on his right cheek. "Amir?" In an instant, the entire family saw him, and none of them were smiling. Without a word, his father put his arm around his mother and led her away. His siblings followed.

He had been expecting a cold reception, and so he tagged along sheepishly. They ignored him until they got to the elevator. His family entered, turned to face him, and as he stepped in, his father held up his hand, and very gently, pushed him back beyond the threshold. When the doors closed, Amir was standing alone, bag in hand, awash in a sea of strangers.

He changed his ticket and went back to the school, riding out the holidays in his dorm room with a handful of others. He drank more than he ever had, and it quickly became a habit. As soon as the school offices opened for business in January, he received a notice that his account had been closed and he would need to vacate his dorm room within the week.

Amir slid into a deep depression that his dependence on alcohol only made worse. He became angry and bitter toward his family and his faith. After several years of menial jobs and barely scraping by, he finished his associate's degree at the local community college. Taking out a painfully large student loan, he once again entered university life as a full-time student.

He found friends again, of course, and felt particularly drawn to the Asian Student Union. He found several people there with stories not too different from his own. He even dated a young Sikh woman a time or two who admired how he had insisted on living his life on his own terms.

Inside, however, he felt like a failure. He had turned his back on everything he had ever been taught one must be or do to be successful, acceptable, good, or noble. He felt like none of those things, and alcohol was, he was finding, a terrible substitute. One day he broke down, and instead of going to school, he just slept. Eventually, in the afternoon, he found his way to the local copy shop owned by a very sweet, elderly Sikh man with the unlikely name of Ned.

Ned asked him why he was so glum, and when he realized Amir really needed to talk, invited him to have a seat in the back room. Ned listened with interest and compassion while Amir bared his soul. Once the young man had exhausted himself, Ned thoughtfully made him a cup of tea. Sitting down again, Ned spoke very gently. "It is very sad about your family—that your parents treated you as they did. They must be hurting as much as you are."

Amir had not thought of that. He was only aware of his own feelings of betrayal. "I don't think they turned their back on you because they are evil people," Ned continued. "I think they did it because they love you and could not stand to see you destroy yourself."

Amir thought that was a load of crap, but he was fond of Ned and so he hung in there and kept talking. "But I didn't destroy myself. I just wanted to feel . . . okay."

"And do you feel 'okay'?"

"No! I feel terrible."

"It is very sad about your family." Ned said again, and then there was a customer to take care of. When Ned returned, he asked, gently, "How do you think God feels?"

Amir had not thought about God's feelings for a very long time. "I'm not sure God has feelings anymore."

"Maybe you are just so numb to your own that you can't imagine them, hmm? I assure you, though, that they are there. And God's feelings are there, too." Amir did not know what to say. "Would you like to know what I think God is feeling?" Amir didn't, really, but he was sure he was about to find out anyway. "I think God does not care about whether you cut your hair or not. I think God does not care about whether you marry the girl your parents have picked out for you. I think God does not care whether you get drunk now and then."

Amir was shocked. He had never heard an elder speak like this. "Here's what I think. I think that God loves you so passionately that there is nothing you could ever do to change his mind, no place you can go to that is too far away that he would stop longing for you, calling to you. God is the Beloved, more intimate than any wife or husband. Nothing you do can ever change that love. There are lots of faithful Muslims that cut their hair. There are lots of Hindus that dance before God's images that do not observe our feasts. There are lots of Sikhs who do not have families to love them. None of them are very different from you. God loves them fiercely, just as fiercely as God loves you. And they love God with their whole heart. Your family may have turned their backs on you, Amir, but the Beloved has not. God did not walk away from you; you walked away from God. But the good news is, he has been following you all the way, only one step behind you, ready to embrace you at any moment. He is always waiting for you to sing the Name."

Ned's words unleashed a flood of emotions that Amir had kept dammed up for some time, and he sobbed with no attempt to control it. When he was quiet, he asked in a whisper, "I don't know how to start again. I've already cut my hair."

"Amir, we don't leave our hair uncut because God will be angry with us if we don't. We do these things out of love for God, not out of fear of Him if we do not. These traditions are human expressions of devotion, not divine commandments. They have to come from your heart, or they mean nothing."

Amir's story is a common one, regardless of one's religious tradition. Often circumstance or personality conflicts within the family can drive Traditional Believers to rebel against what they perceive to be oppressive or outdated beliefs or behaviors. But instead of moving to a more liberal or less intense faith style, they become Jack Believers, estranged from their traditions of origin, yet unable to move beyond them ideologically.

The best option for a Jack Believer is usually to help him or her resolve the conflicts with their religion, which are more often rooted in human fanaticism and intolerance than with the foundational beliefs of the tradition. Just as Amir took the traditional disciplines of the Sikh faith to be divine mandates, his spiritual guide made clear to him that they are human inventions—devotional practices, and nothing more. But if Amir's family is not clear on the distinction, or if they perceive his "rebellion" as being a rejection of them and all they hold dear, Amir could not help but feel rejected by his faith as well as by his family.

The trick is not to appeal to a more liberal interpretation, but to dive down deep into the tradition, to appeal to the most foundational authority available to refute the shunning behavior or other source of conflict. A foundational authority (such as the Torah for Jews, the words of Jesus for Christians, the early Buddhist sutras for Buddhists, etc.) cannot be refuted intellectually, nor waved aside as modern rationalizations. Religious abuse must be met on its own ground and refuted with its own authorities to be useful for Jacks.

The good news is that once a Jack has been restored to his or her community, he or she returns with wisdom impossible to possess prior to his or her exile. From the good graces of the Traditional community, the migrator may or may not proceed to another faith style. Even if they remain in the Traditional camp (as most will), they will be there with more wisdom and compassion than many others who have not strayed, and can serve as leavening influences in their communities.

Jack Believers to Ethical Humanists. The only other choice most Jack Believers have—besides returning to their Traditional communities—is to jettison religion altogether. Leah was raised in an Orthodox Jewish home, which, while close-knit and loving, also seemed to her stifling and abusive in certain respects, especially as she advanced through her teens. She was smart and ambitious and didn't understand why education for women was so frowned upon. She had learned that men and women were equal, but made for different purposes and although outwardly she assented to this, inwardly she felt hurt and resentful. A deep sense of guilt and shame built up in her around this issue, and she fancied herself—to her own horror—more a daughter of Lilith (Adam's first, rebellious wife in Jewish folklore) than of Eve.

She kept most of these thoughts and feelings to herself, however, and agreed to allow the temple matchmaker to find her a husband. She felt no particular attraction to the man picked out for her, but willed herself to give it a chance, and they were married when she was twenty.

It was hell. Very soon, the traditional role of the Jewish wife—always held up as an ideal for Leah—proved to be more than she could bear. Every day as she was tending to her husband's needs, she felt her own untended needs screaming at her. She dismissed these thoughts as selfish at first, and willed them away, but they never went for long. And then one day, after her husband left for work, she packed a suitcase and bought a plane ticket for Los Angeles, clear across the country.

She knew this would make her the scandal of the community, which is why she wanted to get as far away from it as she could. She still, in her heart, believed they were right. But she also knew she could not do it. A fundamental divergence in her psyche pulled her in two different directions simultaneously, and the stress of it was more than she could bear. When she landed in Los Angeles, she sold her grandmother's jewelry, got a small apartment, and a job. She kept her phone number unlisted, and always approached the mailbox with trepidation.

On Sabbath, she would light the candles and say the prayers, but felt like a traitor doing it. One day a co-worker invited her to a lecture at the Society for Humanistic Advancement. She agreed, having no idea what the topic of the lecture would be. She was shocked when the lecturer began speaking on religion as the cause of a host of psychological neuroses.

She related with almost everything the speaker said. He closed his talk by saying that "freedom of religion" meant for him "freedom *from* religion," which was the greatest guarantee of religious freedom this country had to offer. He invited everyone there to throw off the fetters of outdated superstition and to embrace the world as-it-was, asking for no more than this life, and no more elaborate spirituality than simply being a part of the vast and mysterious cosmos.

She fired her God that very night. She signed up for the Society's newsletter and began attending lectures regularly. She also sought out a psychotherapist—a secular Jew who could support her journey. After a short time, she felt empowered and in control of her life for the first time ever. Seizing upon this, she registered at the local community college and started working toward her degree. She put her Sabbath candles in a bottom drawer and instead of going to High Holy Day services that year, went with her friend from work to a week-long silent film festival.

She still felt a twinge of guilt now and then, but with some help from her therapist, she was able to work through these emotions until the pervading feeling of the "rightness" of her new life overshadowed any second thoughts that occasionally popped up. She was eventually served with divorce papers, which she signed, but never did speak to her former husband. Nor did she speak to anyone in her family for many years. By that time, however, she had married that friend from work and was bringing up their first child completely free from any religious dogma. She experienced it as yet another liberation—for her and for her child.

It is not easy for Jack Believers to leave behind the Traditional paradigm. Leah's case is the exception, not the rule. Yet it does happen, and many spiritual guides will have opportunity to encounter and assist people on journeys like hers.

It is hard to overemphasize what a very real salvation leaving one's religion can be. Religious traditions develop over many centuries, encouraging a specific way of being. If one cannot *be* that, a crisis of faith, identity, and usually both will occur. Traditional paradigms overwhelmingly value conformity over exceptionality, and many people who are in any way "exceptional" may have a difficult time feeling as if they belong. For many of them, an enforced (or even willed) conformity with the Tradition is simply not possible. Much easier, for many people, is abandonment of any overtly spiritual practice.

It will be difficult for many spiritual guides to, in good conscience, support someone's retreat from religious life. This is where self-selection on the part of the spiritual guide is of paramount importance. If one cannot support such a journey, then one should not endeavor to work with someone who is on it. All spiritual guides should have a good sense of their own limitations, and should know when to refer a client out.

A spiritual guide who can work with such clients will be one who will see the value of walking away from a religious practice that feels abusive or inauthentic for his or her clients. No spiritual practice is far better than a spiritual practice that diminishes a person's humanity or sense of self.

A person may need to heal from religious wounding before he or she can embrace a healthier spiritual path. But some future reestablishment of a conventional "spiritual" life cannot be the guide's goal, either. It may be that, once liberated from an abusive spirituality, a client will only then fully flower and come into his or her authentic being. They may indeed find a permanent home as an Ethical Humanist. Only a spiritual guide who understands the value and authenticity of the Humanist path, as Leah's therapist no doubt did, will be able to effectively companion such a client.

Afterword

This exploration of the Faith Styles model is just a beginning. It serves as merely an introduction and can only scratch the surface—there is much more to be learned. But that will need to be the subject of other articles or other books. I would be very interested, for instance, to learn what percentage of the U.S. population fits into which of the faith styles—and this will undoubtedly change according to geographic location. Furthermore, a more detailed study might reveal the percentages of each faith style within the various generational populations.

I would also be very interested in the stories that result from those who use the Faith Styles system in their own ministries. How has it been helpful—or not so helpful—for you? Taking care to preserve the anonymity of your clients, please feel free to share your stories with me at jmabry@apocryphile.org. A further collection of case studies may result if enough people share.

I also commend this work to educators, those training spiritual guides, to help their students understand and assess those they work with. I want to hear your stories as well.

Author the Author

The Rev. John R. Mabry, PhD, teaches spiritual direction, world religions, and interfaith theology. He holds a master's degree in creation spirituality and a doctorate in philosophy and religion. He has served as editor of *Creation Spirituality* magazine and *Presence: An International Journal of Spiritual Direction*, and as managing editor for the Episcopal Diocese of California's *Pacific Church News*. He currently serves as co-pastor of Grace North Church in Berkeley, California, a congregational catholic community, and as director of the Interfaith Spiritual Direction Certificate Program at the Chaplaincy Institute for Arts and Interfaith Ministry. His current research includes early Jewish Christian and Gnostic literature, especially the Gospels of Thomas and Philip. Visit his website at www.apocryphile.org/jrm/.